Advance Acclaim for
FRAMEWORKS FOR BUSINESS SUCCESS

"George has a way of taking a very complex and extraordinary topic - the entrepreneurial lifecycle - and simplifying it in a way that every business owner can understand, from the fledgling start-up to the seasoned serial entrepreneur. He balances execution, operations, finance and more with real-life examples the reader can grab onto and apply to their circumstances. Building a company right from the start with your exit in mind is a framework for success. Well done, George!" – Steve Conwell, CEO, Final Ascent LLC.

"Great book for the any business owner, especially someone considering opening a business or has just started one. George laid out all of the aspects of effectively running a company in an easy to read and understand format." – Tim Kiernan, 360 Consulting

"*Frameworks for Business Success* is a must read for any business owner. Mr. Mayfield provides amazing insight into the necessities of a functional business. *Frameworks for Business Success* puts an entire college level Business Management course work into one book and provides the insight to run and grow a successful business. Whether you did or didn't get your degree in business administration / management, this book is the go-to guide for success!" – John Beaty, CBPA, Insperity

"No matter your level of business knowledge or what stage your business is currently in, read this book! The steps are easy to understand and simple (not easy) to implement.
If you're serious about building, running, and maintaining your business machine, the principles and procedures in this book must be implemented. I wish I could have read this book when I started my business career almost 40 years ago." – Eric Harrison, 4impact Data, Author of Amazon Best-selling book, *Mustard Seed Faith*

"To take your business to the next level, or even if you are just starting out, "*Frameworks for Business Success*" is a must read. Building your business is a top priority and this is the roadmap to get you there." – Rob Bliss, CEO, Purple Cow Branding

"I highly recommend reading George Mayfield's *Frameworks for Business Success* to business owners all over the world! It provides simple yet effective strategies and techniques that are essential in today's global market. This book has made an impact on how I run my business in Turkey, and I am sure it can do the same for you!" – Sezen Inci, Owner, Istabul Dog Academy

"I thoroughly enjoyed reading *Frameworks for Business Success*! George's approach to teaching is intriguing and thought-provoking; his stories were engaging and compelling and sometimes funny. I definitely encourage anyone starting a company or even a person looking to restructure their business to read this book." – Ieshea Hollins, PMP®, M-PM, CISO; Founder/CEO of Direnzic Technology

"I read *Frameworks for Business Success* expecting just another generic 'how to achieve success' book. George gives business fundamentals a human element and lets you know the 'why' and the 'how'. If you are trying to start a new business or grow your current business buy this book and create your own framework to success!!" – Chris Honeycutt, Texas Security Bank

Frameworks

For

Business Success

How to Scale your Business from

Entrepreneur to Enterprise

to Build an

Increasingly

Profitable Company

George Mayfield

Frameworks Consortium Publishing
Frisco, TX 75035

Frameworks Consortium Publishing can bring authors to your live event. For more information or to book an event contact speaking@frameworksconsortiumpublishing.com

For information about special discounts for bulk purchases, please contact orders@frameworksconsortiumpublishing.com

Mayfield, George R.
        Frameworks for Business Success: How to Scale Your Business from Entrepreneur to Enterprise to Build an Increasingly Profitable Company / by George Mayfield
                ISBN: 978-1-960225-02-3 (Hardcover)
                ISBN: 978-1-960225-03-0 (Paperback)
                ISBN: 978-1-960225-04-7 (eBook-Kindle)

Subjects: LCSH: Small Business Growth | Business Strategy | Mastermind | Entrepreneurship

                Library of Congress Control Number: 2023903976

Cover Design by: Sunshine Vizconde
Foreword by: Craig Duswalt
Chapter Logos Design by: Sunshine Vizconde
Photography Credits: Lanay Renstrom

Printed in the United States of America

www.FrameworksForBusinessSuccess.com

To all those who have started a great business from nothing, especially those dealing with personal hardships. I commend you for your great resilience, strength, and determination.

Contents

Foreword

By Craig Duswalt

Hello, and welcome to the book, *Frameworks For Business Success*, by George Mayfield. In this book, you will find powerful and actionable advice for business owners looking to take their business to the next level.

I met George a few years ago and was immediately inspired by his ambition and drive. His commitment to helping others, no matter the cost, is something that I have admired in his profession. I have witnessed him teach the importance of not only providing value but also connecting with those around us to build lasting relationships. This is why I believe George will continue to be an invaluable asset for professionals all over the world for many years to come.

It's clear why so many people look up to George as a leader—his trailblazing spirit, unyielding dedication and limitless potential are exemplary characteristics of a true business champion. It is my great pleasure to share this admiration for George, who demonstrates that success can be achieved with hard work and the courage to do what's right.

Throughout my career, I have had the privilege and honor of touring with some of the most iconic names in music, such as Guns N' Roses and Air Supply. When I wasn't on tour, I was running my own successful ad firm and speaking at events around the country on topics such as outside-the-box marketing and mindset. My background has allowed me to understand what it takes to promote yourself and your business in creative ways, which is why I am so excited to be writing a foreword for George Mayfield's book Frameworks for Business Success.

When it comes to building a successful business, the key is to focus on the fundamentals. Having a solid plan and well-defined goals are essential components for achieving success in any industry. However, many entrepreneurs often overlook one of the most important elements of their business - establishing strong frameworks that will ensure they have long-term success. George Mayfield has done an amazing job of outlining the essential components that can help entrepreneurs create a foundation for their business and lay out the steps needed to make it successful.

It is my belief that everyone should use frameworks as part of their overall strategy. They will serve as a roadmap for your plans and provide important guidance on how to achieve success. In Frameworks for Business Success, George Mayfield provides great insight into the fundamentals of business framework building and what it takes to be successful in almost any industry. This book is not necessarily for those who are just starting on their entrepreneurial journey, although there is plenty of valuable advice that can help you understand your future self. It's primarily targeted at established businesses who already have a good foundation but need a bit of help to get over the hurdle at the 3-5 million in revenue point and really start growing their business.

George Mayfield's book tackles the subject of scaling a business head-on, providing readers with in-depth insights on what makes a business successful and how to develop effective strategies that can lead to lasting success. Not only does he discuss topics such as creating joint ventures and understanding compliance regulations, but George also explains why it is so important to get advice from experienced professionals before making decisions. His knowledge and expertise are invaluable, and his guidance can help aspiring entrepreneurs make the right choices to ensure their businesses will thrive.

The Power of Mindset

When it comes to succeeding in any endeavor, one of the most important elements is mindset. As a professional speaker, I have seen how businesses can grow when you believe in yourself and your abilities. It doesn't matter how much skill or knowledge you have if your mindset isn't right. This book provides invaluable information on how to develop a winning mindset no matter what type of business you are running. As an entrepreneur myself, I understand that there will inevitably be challenges along the way, but with the right attitude you can face those challenges head-on and come out on top.

Being a RockStar is an incredibly demanding job. From writing and recording music to organizing tours and promotional events, it takes a lot of hard work, dedication, and commitment to be successful in this role. But perhaps one of the most important elements for success is having the right mindset. A RockStar must ensure that they are mentally prepared to lead their group through all the ups and downs that come with being part of a rock band. This means developing positive attitudes towards challenges, staying focused on goals, maintaining motivation levels throughout long hours of practice or performance time, and fostering strong relationships between members within the group.

In order to succeed as a RockStar, it's essential to have an optimistic outlook on any situation you find yourself facing in your musical journey. No matter how difficult things may seem at times or how many obstacles arise along the way, it's important not to give up hope but instead stay motivated by working hard even if progress seems slow going. Focusing on small successes can help build confidence so that when bigger hurdles arrive you will be more likely to overcome them with grace and poise instead of feeling overwhelmed or discouraged by them.

Moreover, RockStars must also work to build a strong team dynamic among their members. This means providing support and encouragement when necessary and ensuring that everyone feels appreciated for the contributions they make to the group. It's important not to overlook individual strengths, as each member has something unique to offer that can help the group reach its goals. By developing an environment of trust and respect, RockStars will be able to cultivate a positive atmosphere within their group which in turn can lead to better performances and a more successful career as a whole.

Being the leader of a business, a "RockStar" in your business, is similar. I believe that the mindset of its leadership is the most important factor in any successful business, and I teach this within my mastermind group. You will need the right mindset to lead your team, focus on goals and stay motivated no matter what. Additionally, you must build a team dynamic that emphasizes trust and respect for all employees. With the right attitude in place, you can create an environment of success and growth for your business.

George Mayfield's book provides invaluable advice on how to develop these key elements for success so that entrepreneurs can reach their full potential and scale their businesses with ease. By reading this book, aspiring business owners can gain the knowledge needed to make informed decisions and take advantage of every opportunity presented to them. With George's help, readers can take control of their future and achieve great things!

Operational Guidance

In addition to focusing on developing the right mindset, this book also provides useful operational guidance on growing your business. From understanding the importance of customer service and market research to learning how to utilize social media effectively, this book covers all of these topics in detail so that entrepreneurs can gain a better understanding of how best to run their businesses.

When I toured with world-renowned bands, I had to make sure our performance logistics were always on point so that the show would go off without a hitch. Our band's manager and team understood the various operational tasks associated with being part of a rock band. This includes things like setting up rehearsal spaces, purchasing instruments and sound equipment, booking shows and tours, creating promotional materials such as posters or flyers, and even managing finances when necessary. All these activities require careful planning in order for them to be completed efficiently and effectively. Additionally, it's important for the leader of any group to maintain good communication between members so that everyone knows what their role is within the organization and how they can contribute most effectively towards achieving their goals.

Aside from simply knowing what needs to be done operationally speaking on any given day or week; however, effective leaders must also know how best to do those tasks while still maintaining high standards throughout the process. This means taking the time to understand and appreciate each member of your team, their individual strengths and weaknesses, as well as delegating tasks appropriately in order to ensure that everyone is doing what they're best at. Additionally, it also requires having a clear vision for where you want the organization to go and communicating that vision effectively so that everyone is on board with achieving it. By focusing on developing these key elements throughout your career you can build strong relationships within your team and set yourself up for success no matter what environment you are operating within.

These fundamental operational frameworks are important to a business owner, too. When I'm teaching within my mastermind group, we focus on developing a plan of action that works for each person in order to make sure they are set up for success.

Essentially, the more you understand about what it takes to have a successful business the further ahead you will be when putting your own plans into effect. George Mayfield provides readers with all the information needed to build their operations from the ground up and develop their own unique approach towards running their businesses efficiently and effectively. The systems outlined in this book can help any individual reach their full potential and succeed as an entrepreneur.

* * *

As a business owner, you understand that success is not something that happens overnight. It takes hard work and dedication, not only from yourself but from your team as well. George's book helps you with proven strategies for creating valuable frameworks so you can build a lasting foundation for success in your business.

He explores what exactly a business framework is, how to strengthen it through key performance indicators (KPIs), and how to create realistic goals and strategies tailored specifically to your business. He also delves into the importance of bringing on an experienced Board of Advisors and how best to incorporate their advice into the decision-making process. Additionally, he covers topics like project budgeting and change management so that progress can be tracked effectively while still allowing room for unexpected surprises along the way.

One of the things I respect about George is that he understands that managing a successful business takes more than just numbers; it takes an understanding of people and processes, and you must consider the world outside your business. That's why he discusses topics like executive retreats, wellness programs, creating shared value and more; all designed with the intent of powering up both yourself and your team members so that everyone involved can reach their fullest potential. George also helps you to look at planning for future growth including creating contingency plans in case of emergencies or unexpected events such as rapid company expansion or even a planned exit strategy should you decide the time has come to move on from your current venture.

No matter your motivation for picking up this book—whether it's building new structures within an existing business or starting one from scratch—I hope that investing some time into reading his words of wisdom will result in tangible improvements within your own enterprise!!

Deliver Your Message Like a RockStar

About Craig Duswalt

Craig Duswalt is a Professional Keynote Speaker, Author, Podcaster, and the creator of the brands RockStar Marketing and Rock Your Life. Craig has written 11 books and is a multiple #1 Amazon Best-Selling Author.

Craig's background includes touring with Guns N' Roses, as Axl Rose's personal assistant, and Air Supply, as the band's personal assistant.

Craig was also an award-winning copywriter, working as a Creative Director for a Los Angeles-based ad agency until opening up his own ad agency, Green Room Design & Advertising, which was named the 2002 Santa Clarita Valley Chamber of Commerce Small Business of the Year.

Craig combined his backgrounds in both music and marketing, and is now a professional speaker and author, promoting his Rock Your Life Events all over the country, teaching Corporate

America, entrepreneurs, small businesses, home-based business and the self-employed how to "Deliver Their Message Like A RockStar."

Craig's Rock Your Life Events take place every Spring and Fall in Dallas and Los Angeles.

Craig delivers a very high-energy presentation, filled with useable content, interesting videos, exciting music, and extremely unique (never heard before) stories from his days touring with Guns N' Roses and Air Supply, and his days working with corporate giants including Baskin Robbins, Los Angeles Dodgers, ESPN, and the Academy Awards just to name a few.

Craig speaks to corporations, and at numerous conferences, associations and networking groups, teaching what it takes to become known as an expert and an influencer amongst clients and potential customers.

"The trick is learning to frame your new ideas as tweaks of old ideas, to mix a little fluency with a little disfluency—to make your audience see the familiarity behind the surprise."

— Derek Thompson, Hit Makers: The Science of Popularity in an Age of Distraction

Framing

Running a business is hard. There are many conditions that need to come together near perfectly to make a business even remotely successful. It must have the right leadership, the right market, the right economy, the right team, the right culture, the right tools, the right amount of capital, and it must be the right time. All those things have to work together in the right way and if any one of those things are missing or not a fit, your business could suffer or even fail altogether. Many of these things can't even be directly controlled. It's an outright miracle that any business exists!

Many great business books touch on any one of those conditions or even a mixture of a few. How to market, how to raise capital, how to build a winning team -- all those are great things to know and work on in your business. Perhaps you've already read some of those books. Maybe you've brought in a consultant to help with one or two of those things.

While one area in your business might have improved, you found yourself worrying about something else. Like a circus act, you find yourself spinning plates on the end of a stick. You're constantly moving from one plate to another, just making sure that each one is spinning fast enough to stay level before you move to the next, continuously revisiting them all over and over. Spend too much time on one, and you'll find that another has crashed to the floor.

What does a company that is spinning plates look like? Every couple of months, there is a new initiative. For a while, they may have weekly meetings, but those eventually fall off the calendar. They develop a playbook, but employees stop following it once they realize no one is holding them to it. They would buy a CRM that doesn't get properly used anymore. The business is propped up on the backs of just a few employees who, for one reason or another, stick it out. These are the people in the company who are spinning plates and keeping the company going.

The number of businesses that fail in the first 5 years is staggering, but it makes unfortunate sense. Many entrepreneurs believe that they can control those business conditions through sheer willpower alone. Some don't know what those conditions are or what they need to be. They don't know what to look for nor how to create a business environment that fosters success. They make it by as long as they can on luck; capital from a previous job or property sale, strong local network of potential customers, or perhaps a readymade cheap employment source found in their family members. They don't understand that those elements aren't necessarily replicable and attribute that luck to skill or business viability and that becomes their downfall.

A business may make it past 5 years because the owner or leadership compensated awareness of those business conditions with hard work. They would work endless hours every week, foregoing vacations and even family events. They would lie in bed stressing about finances, employee issues, or just what their next tactic should be. They would constantly change how they market or how they hire or how they deliver their business to their clients. They, themselves, are spinning plates.

At some point the business owner realizes that this isn't scalable, and it isn't the reason they got into business. The business owner now faces the problem of how to scale their business, gain more market share, increase their revenue, and reach their own goals of being able to enjoy all the wealth that has come from the value put into a business. They begin to realize that spinning plates is not going to work and that they can't keep doing what they've been doing and expect better results.

This book aims to provide business owners with a clear understanding of how to navigate the chaos and get out of the weeds. It will help you assess all areas of your business and how they function together. Additionally, it will teach you how to view external factors that shape the future of your company and use that knowledge to develop a successful strategy. Moreover, it offers insights on how you, as a business owner, interact with your company and how to ensure that you are ethically extracting the value you've worked hard to build for yourself and your family.

Ultimately, this book aims to provide business owners with a clear understanding of what it takes to build and sustain a successful business. It will help you identify the areas that need improvement and equip you with the tools necessary for success. By leveraging these skills, you will be able to move beyond spinning plates and into creating long-term sustainable systems that will make your business thrive.

Business frameworks are essential for successful businesses. They are tried and true practices and concepts that help a business control, induce, and regulate business conditions that result in success. They provide structure, organization, and guidance to help businesses operate more effectively and efficiently. They define roles, responsibilities, and processes within the organization, enabling the business to focus on what it does best for its clients. Business owners need not be spinning plates anymore, but instead commit to changing the way they think about business.

It takes a special kind of mind to see the internal operations of a business as well as the external factors that make up these business conditions and orchestrate them in a way that fosters success. They must integrate and control the various activities within a business while anticipating changes in the business environment. They must know how to use business frameworks to create systems and processes that are robust, effective, and sustainable.

* * *

I was born and raised in a small Texas town a little over an hour away from the Dallas Fort Worth metroplex. My family wasn't well off, but my father worked hard to pay bills and take the occasional humble vacation, usually a camping trip. He had a full-time job but worked nearly every evening and weekend on other projects.

My dad worked at a factory that made ventilation products for as far back as I could remember. He was the company's Chief Engineer, yet he never got his high school diploma. He designed a lot of the products still sold today and ran the machine shop that built some of the machines that created the products.

He had always been a sort of Jack of all trades. Though he learned a lot from his dad, he continued to teach himself new skills. He taught himself how to use drafting software. He could weld exceptionally well, do plumbing, electrician work, roofing, cabinetry…the list goes on. He would pick up hobbies like building smokers and smoking brisket, bicycling, or creating metal figurines out of pipe tubing. He even took up cake decorating for a while.

He wasn't one of those guys that could do a lot of things but be a master of none of them. Everything he did, he was exceptionally proficient in, and he would do it big! That brisket he smoked? He built a huge smoker trailer and sold brisket on

5

the side of a busy road to donate to a non-profit. He catered for several company and social events. Cake decorating? He made very unique cakes and confections (utilizing what he knew about carpentry, dry wall, and other skills) and sold them for weddings and birthdays. He created hundreds of figurines from welded pipe materials and took them to the local trade fair to sell.

People sought him out when they had a really strange problem that needed to be solved and wanted the highest quality work. I didn't always know who they were or their significance, but many times I found myself at some famous person's house, bringing my dad tools and cleaning up after the job.

I'd like to say I was amazed at the stuff he could do, but I didn't know him any other way. To that point, I didn't know my family any other way. It wasn't just my dad. My aunt did the same thing. She would sew country style anthropomorphic stuffed animals, build furniture, or wood crafts to sell on the weekends after her day job. My grandfather ran a boot sales and repair shop for several decades. My cousin ran a small car dealership. Another cousin ran a restaurant. Another family member trained cutting horses (that doesn't mean what it sounds like!).

Entrepreneurism runs deep in my family. Long ago, there was even a town called Mayfield Switch. It was founded as a train stop town where people would gather goods to be sent for sale in Ft. Worth or brought in to stock the town's general store. It was since renamed to Clairette, but I still have many relatives that live nearby operating their own business.

One thing that I noticed growing up in a family like this is that while these extraordinary people could do amazing things and provide a great value to others, some of them struggled with running a business consistently.

My father earned enough money to put food on the table, but his business allowed us enough to have slightly better food on the table. He worked a lot. 7am to 4:30 pm at the manufacturing plant, then 5pm till 8, 9, or 10 in the evening every weekday. Then, even longer every weekend. I knew because I was there alongside him – Myself and my brother.

We were expected to either ride the school bus to the area of town where he was working or ride our bikes. We would have to carry work clothes with us throughout the day at school. My father, brother, and I would work until the sun went down and the work lights attracted too many bugs to see what we were doing. Later, we'd get home, take a shower, and then do any homework we had for the day. To be honest, I was usually too tired to care about homework. My grades suffered, of course. It was a middle-class cycle of working hard for mediocrity.

I was proud of the hard work my dad was doing for us, but I knew there was something better. I remember many arguments with my dad. I'd argue that there was a better way and he'd tell me the only way is through hard work. He'd call me lazy, and I'd think him foolish, though I almost never dared say it and was never really sure I meant it.

***

The hometown I was raised in had some wonderful individuals, yet daily life tended to be mundane and monotonous. There wasn't a lot of new things going on. Staring out the car window as a kid or riding my bike through the town, I'd see many homes and buildings that didn't seem fit to live in. I saw yards full of old cars. I saw road ditches full of beer cans and trash. Through my childhood eyes, I saw a town that was full of people that had given up.

In my hometown, people found work in a few factories. My dad worked at the ventilation company, while there was also a brick factory, box factory and pressurized tank facility. Additionally, numerous small businesses were based in our town's converted Vietnam War era army base - these included glass-making companies to cabinet makers.

Every day I observed people getting off work, their sweat-drenched and greasy clothing. Defeated and defeated again, they'd line up at the store to buy a six pack of beer - drowning away in misery. I never really judged these people, but I knew then that this wasn't a life I wanted for myself; instead, my goal was always something much higher.

I distanced myself from this lifestyle. Whatever I saw people doing, I'd do the opposite. Country music? No, Classical. Ripped jeans? No, slacks. In a small town in the 80s, I was a kid wearing home-made button up shirts, listening to Beethoven, and reading every advanced book I could get my hands on in the school library. And, oh, man, did I pay for it! Every bully in town had his mark on me.

I was one of the top students in music. I could beat anyone in "name that tune"! In sixth grade, we were introduced to band class. On the first day of class, I made my way to the classroom, which was in a small building leftover from the old school that the new one had been built next to. A sign on the door said to stand in line until the band director arrived. I was third in line.

Suddenly, the door swung open, and the band director pointed a finger at the first person in line.

"What do you want to play?"

"Trumpet", said the first kid.

"Fourth row, sit."

Another finger, "What do you want to play?"

The second kid said, "Drums"

"Back row, sit."

The band director rounded on me… I froze. I had no idea. I was just figuring this out. I was expecting a tour or lesson on what band even was. I wasn't prepared.

"What's the most elegant instrument", I thought. "Violin? Yes".

"Violin" I said.

"This is band, not orchestra." He said coldly." What do you want to play?"

Oh… I thought back to the classical music I listened to. The soundtracks. The harsh and woodsy sound that permeated through the Jurassic Park soundtrack that I liked.

"Flute?"

"First row, sit."

After I sat down, I watched the room fill out. It didn't take long before I realized the mistake I had made. I got up and went back to the door and was told to sit down again. I didn't. I stood by the band director's desk until the room was full. The metal door slammed shut as the director whisked into the room towards his desk.

"What do you want?" he asked. I told him that I wanted to change instruments.

"What you chose is done. Sit.", he said.

I had dug my grave. I had given every bully a nuclear bomb for the next six years to make fun of and pummel me out of existence. While every other band kid proudly carried their instrument from class to class and on the school bus home, I was carrying my books while my flute case was shoved into my backpack. My desire to be different from everybody was my own fault.

***

But I was different. And those differences helped me to sit back and view the world differently. They allowed me to make observations in the world that many could not – or would not see.

I made friends as time went on. People matured and some stood up for me. Most had moved into town rather than being born there. John, Andy, and Jared helped me realize that I wasn't weird. That all these observations I had made weren't wrong – that the principles I had developed weren't totally based on error. They helped me learn that by being odd, I had a strength that most did not.

I saw the strengths in my friends, too. John was highly artistic. Andy was super smart about the way the world worked. Jared was intrinsically intelligent about random things that turned out to be not really random at all. I saw a strength in all of us together. With the principles I had made over the years, I saw how our strengths could combine to make something better. Something that could benefit anyone else who wanted something better. Things that the school didn't offer. I formed an organization with the three of us: The Spam Eaters of Yugoslavia.

We didn't eat Spam and none of us had ever been to Yugoslavia. We borrowed from our love of Monty Python and a random country on an outdated globe. This organization started to grow immediately. It turned out that there were more people like us. People who were trying to stand out from the grain. People who were trying to be something better than what they were born into.

We had no idea what we were doing, but we were raising students up. We were all now part of something. We were above the bullies. We were above oppressive teachers, even. We succeeded.

With our efforts, we were successful in stopping a proposed school policy that would require students to wear ID badges, visible at all times, in a lanyard around their necks. We didn't want to walk around like drones in a corporation, and because of our strength, we made sure it wasn't passed.

***

I left town as soon as I could. No one in my family has ever gone to college and there's no way we could have ever afforded it. There was no way I was going to get stuck "working in the factory". I signed up for the Navy in my Junior year. After my senior year, I didn't even wait a week.

In the Navy, I was alone again. I had to figure out adult life by myself. I chose to be a machinist, just like my dad. I put myself in the same group of people who would make fun of me for reading books. I was at square one.

I began again to observe the world around me. Why did things work the way that they did? I observed that a great deal of our processes was unbelievably inefficient. We squandered resources on repainting items we would soon replace, scheduling watches without purpose, and not providing appropriate instruction for tasks.

Not even the leadership would back me up most of the time. I never got in trouble, per se, but I was known as the guy who couldn't just work without questioning authority. I was so different from those around me that I learned years later that most of my shipmates thought I was with NCIS and sent to investigate anything that might have been going on.

Still, I had gotten leadership experience and was one day chosen to lead a tiger team throughout the ship to catalog damage control equipment. We made a list of all the fire extinguishers, battery-powered lighting, emergency doorways, and other equipment. Soon, I began looking at our findings.

Some of it made perfect sense. Corrosion of equipment that had exposure to the elements? Sure. Others, not so much. I began to apply my observations to the data. Some of these spaces were indoors, but the maintenance for this equipment was under the authority of people who held jobs in Intelligence, IT, or supporting administration. I took my findings to a chief who listened as I explained what I thought was going on.

My hypothesis was that the people in charge of maintenance in their spaces may have instructions on how to carry out the tasks, but not the aptitude to understand why or the nuances that may come with it. "Replace bad rubber" is a good instruction, but it assumes that the reader knows what bad rubber looks like.

And with that, I was put in charge of a larger team of people. As per my suggestion, the captain of the ship had created a larger team that was composed of people from all the ship's divisions. Our mission was to learn by doing. Over the next couple of months, we were able to fix about 70% of the damage control equipment before we arrived back in the United States. This saved millions of dollars as an alternative to having shipyard contractors replace the equipment and helped spur a paradigm shift in the way that maintenance was carried out on the ship.

Seeing the potential, I was faced with becoming an officer or leaving the Navy after my commitment and getting a college degree. I loved serving our country, but my decision was quickly made.

Through my experience in college, I couldn't help but think back to the experiences I had growing up in my small hometown. I was infatuated with the business theories from people like Michael Porter, Gerard Hofstede, Fred Fielder, and others. I felt like I had discovered a gold mine of information.

The more I learned about business, the more I realized how I could help entrepreneurs like those in my family. I decided that I wanted to help business owners with what they didn't know. I wanted to empower extraordinary people to be able to scale their abilities so that they could add even more value to their communities.

As a result, I tailored my career around comprehending how firms can use proven principles to become productive and maximize their profits. Consulting renowned corporations in the industry gave me insight into what successful organizations do correctly and where others falter. Incorporating the wisdom I acquired from these experiences, I created a program that aids business leaders in scaling up further. With this in mind, I designed my practice to assist business owners with prioritizing value over exchanging time for money, while still allowing them the liberty to put functional tasks in place that can help them achieve more success than they could alone.

I continue to think at scale. There's a lot of companies out there that are struggling. And there are a lot of vendors out there that can help in some small or large way, but they're usually all just in it for them. There's got to be a way to bring everyone in together to help each other thrive and grow in whatever conditions the economy throws at us.

Whether a company is a small business or a large corporation, the consistent implementation of business frameworks is the key to finding success. It was that realization that led me to start my own consultancy and build the Frameworks Consortium.

What is a business framework?

A business framework is a model that your business would use for strategic planning, tactical evaluation, and even day to day operations. A business framework would typically set out your goals, how you intend to achieve those goals, and what metrics or indicators you will use to see if you are on track. If you have ever developed a business plan, you've likely used several frameworks to access the market and describe your strategy. If you haven't, reach out to Frameworks Consortium and we'll help!

There are many different business frameworks that can be used depending on the industry and type of organization. One example of a popular business framework is the "lean startup" model, which focuses on iterative and incremental growth to test hypotheses about the market. This framework is often used by tech startups in order to reduce risk and speed up the product development process.

Another popular framework is Porter's five forces, which was developed by business strategist Michael Porter to assess the competitive landscape of an industry. This framework analyzes the external factors that can affect a company's success, such as the bargaining power of suppliers and customers, the level of competition in the industry, and the threat of new entrants.

Harvard Business School, 2022. https://www.isc.hbs.edu/strategy/business-strategy/Pages/the-five-forces.aspx

There are many other business frameworks out there, each of which can be useful for different types of businesses. The frameworks we will cover in this book, however, are foundational to scaling your business success and thinking less like a startup entrepreneur and more like an enterprise company. These essential frameworks will help you identify your standing, anticipate potential problems, remediate gaps, and stay ahead of the competition.

This is crucial for any business, regardless of size and industry, as it will give you a better understanding of how your business is performing and what steps you need to take to achieve success.

It is recommended that businesses implement these frameworks as early as possible in their development cycle. Many times, I have seen potential clients that want to wait until they get that next big client or wait until they have a big team to manage. Oftentimes, that may be too late. Companies like that tend to scale bad habits or sign on clients that take them away from their core competencies. This sets your company up for failure.

If you want to be successful and grow your business, it is essential to implement these frameworks early on. This will not only give your company a better chance for long-term success, but it will also allow you to build a strong foundation and set realistic expectations from the beginning.

The business owner

This book is intended for business owners, executives, and those that strive to someday be one or both. Since you are reading this book, you're likely facing some sort of roadblocks in the business, and you hope this book can help.

The situation that I find most clients in is that they have grown a business past startup and have been operating for 3 – 10 years. They have at least a small team of employees that help the business run the day-to-day activities. They have a decent number of clients bringing in revenue. Yet, the company is uneasy.

Employees are showing signs of unhappiness. They have been patient and loyal for a while. They know that the company has potential to grow, and they believe in you. They also believe that you'll take care of them once the company really kicks off. In the meantime, they haven't been getting paid very well for their work and they may start to wonder if that hard work and loyalty really will pay off. Employees that always showed up early are starting to just barely show up on time. That employee that would clean up around the office now hasn't done that in months. When you have a company-wide holiday party, some don't show up or leave early just after the gifts have been given out.

Your clients feel it, too. There's a certain uncomfortableness with some of your clients. You know that your company isn't really offering the level of service you used to provide them or you're working overtime to bridge the gap that your employees are leaving behind. You dread when the phone rings, knowing that it is more likely a client with an issue that you'll have to take care of. Client turnover may just be keeping up with new clients. As many clients as you bring on, you may feel like some of them are slipping through your fingers.

You feel like you did when you were just starting out. The anxiousness, the worry, the tiredness. Your company is bringing in revenue, but you're not seeing much of it. "Where is it all going?", you often think, looking back at your statements and accounts. You look at your costs, but there's nothing you can really cut. You want to negotiate better pricing on some of them, but you know it really won't move the needle very far. Plus, you just don't have the time.

You're working long hours. Nights, weekends, even holidays, you spend working. Your family life suffers, your hobbies are forgotten. You know that you need to make this right, but that takes time, too. You try to spend some time to strategize, but your brain seems like it's in a fog.

Maybe you've even brought in a coach for a while. They come in for a session, you vent your frustrations and that seems to help. They have you and your team do some personality quizzes, which seems to help explain some things. You have a "rah-rah" session, and everyone is happy. They may tell you that you need to document your processes, shore up your strategy, and hire only the best people, then finger-gun themselves out the door after you give them their check.

But after a time, you realize that they are just telling you to do what you may already know you need to do, and they haven't been successful at helping you find the time to do any of it. You begin to feel like they were just giving you more homework and leaving you to do it alone in your office, after hours. You never finish that strategy, or if you do, it never really gets implemented. Your team goes right back to doing what they were doing and what's worse is they now know that you aren't doing what the coach said either.

> *Note: A business coach isn't a bad idea but not all are equal. This book will show you how a coach can be an integrated part of your business frameworks.*

You may be experiencing some or all these things in your business. It's stressful and it's depressing. You had a dream for your business, and it seems like it is out of reach. Let me help you build the frameworks to take your business to the success you want!

In this book, I guarantee that you'll find at least three invaluable pieces of advice. that will help you. It may be something new, something forgotten, or something said in a new way that makes you realize that a particular thing needs to change. If you want to make a claim on that warranty, my email is at the end of this book. My team will coach you through your problem or refund your money!

Now that I really have your attention, let's get in the mindset. There are two main categories of readers for this book. There's the Adventurer and the Investor. You may find yourself in either extreme or somewhere down the middle. Most business owners are a mixture of both. These aren't personality types and there's no test I'm including so you can find out which one you are. These are simple generalities from my experience.

The Adventurer values experiences. They started their business because it seemed fun. A nine to five job is monotonous. They wanted to be in control of their own destiny and build something great. They wanted to create an environment that people want to be in. They view employees almost as friends.

Reports bore the Adventurer. Processes aren't documented in their business. If they're being honest, it's because it's just sooo boring. But what they'll tell people is that it's just not their skill set, they don't have time, or that the processes are so obvious, anyone should be able to pick it up.

Adventurers love the clients that create a little bit of "positive" chaos. A request for a new feature or a new joint venture idea is a welcome distraction from the daily responsibilities. The Adventurer will take that lunch meeting and the excitement of the new prospect will buzz around the office for the next week. The Adventurer hates being bogged down in business.

Adventurers are going to struggle with a few areas of this book, but there's other areas that will get them absolutely jazzed. The thought of a mastermind is like a club of instant friends that can be a business expense. An executive retreat is a vacation with an excuse. The Adventurer may get through this book quicker just to get to those sections.

The Investor values ROI. Everything they do is calculated. They started their business because they saw a value that wasn't being provided and an opportunity to make more money for themselves than working for someone else. Everything in their business is accounted for and employees are seen mostly as tools to get the job done.

The Investor likely does their own accounting or has a very close eye on who keeps them. They work long hours because it keeps the expenses down. They know which clients are most lucrative and turn away others who aren't when they can get away with it.

The Investor is going to shrink back at certain aspects of this book as well. A Mastermind group seems like a waste of time, as will the executive retreat. "Business isn't supposed to be fun", they may think. They will see a lot of value in reports, key performance indicators, and process improvement. These things help prove the need for their business and show them areas to improve.

Now, both business owners are right. As we'll discuss, adding others to your business can help you enjoy your business more. Bringing in experts will help in making better decisions and help you with your business frameworks. The better vetted your frameworks are, the more value they will bring to your company. The better your business runs, the more you can focus on the parts that are exciting for you AND create more value.

How bad do you want it?

I've made one guarantee in this book so far: that you will find at least three things that can help your business be successful. However, nothing in this book will help you if you aren't determined to make a change and put those things in place. You must make a commitment first to yourself then to your team and your clients. Without that commitment, there's not a single business book, consultant, or coach that can help you be successful.

What works for small businesses and startups doesn't work for long term success (even if you plan to stay small). Businesses that can stay in business the first five years usually succeed through a combination of luck, entrepreneurial spirit, and hard work from the business owners. That isn't to say those aren't important. A Business should try to keep those things as long as possible. But they aren't scalable. Luck will run out, statistically speaking. Entrepreneurial spirit will eventually be exercised. Business Owners' hard work ethic doesn't transfer to employees.

As a business grows, the same things that allowed the business to take off now make a business chaotic. As the entrepreneur, you worked long hours. You couldn't afford to pay for help. Everything was in your head. There wasn't time or a need to document what you were doing and what your plans for the future are. You needed to get clients and perform the service or product delivery tasks – your plan was likely to just keep doing that! Then, you might have hired an employee or two. They might have been your friend or family member. They already had some idea of what you were doing and why. You showed them what you were doing. For the most part, that's what they did, too. They learned by doing.

Then, you hired a few more employees. Sure, some of them are focused on one job. A salesperson, an accountant, someone to answer phone calls. But still they wore multiple hats. It's just what you've got to do in the first few years. It's a bit chaotic, but it gets the job done.

However, you need to work to reduce this chaos as the business grows. There's a point in the business that entrepreneurship just isn't an appropriate way to keep running the business. Bootstraps get worn out - you can't do as much with so little and still be effective. Multiple hats make for a heavy head. You can't hold people accountable when they have too many responsibilities. At some point you must make the commitment to run your business more like a choreographed ice show and less like a hockey match.

Getting out of entrepreneurialism and into enterprise takes hard work. That's something you're likely used to. But you must change your mindset and stop working so hard in your business and instead work just as hard on your business. I know you're exhausted. You've worked so hard for so long. I know you're ready to start enjoying what you've worked for. You started with nothing and built something great, maybe better than you ever expected. At least to some extent, it's a proven concept now. The mountain representing business success is higher than you realize, and you aren't at the top yet. If you try to coast, you'll just lose momentum. Worse, you may start to drift back down.

***

I worked with a business services company where the owner of the company, Sean, functioned as the lead salesperson. The owner knew that to grow his company, he needed to rely more on his employees and less on himself. So, he focused on sales and left the service delivery part of the company up to his team. He hired a very smart guy, Tim, with decades of experience to be the COO.

He celebrated when he would sign 3 or 4 new clients each quarter, but they also lost clients just as fast. Each time a client would threaten to leave, Sean would hold a meeting, bringing in Tim and some of his top performers. They would go over past emails and service requests to try to find the root of the problem. Usually, the meeting would end up with just Sean and Tim. They would have a talk until Sean felt like Tim got the message. There might even be one or two new rules or policies out of it.

The employees worked hard, but most of them did a little bit of everything. The clients they had were very needy, and there were always projects going on. New clients had high expectations based on what Sean had told them in the sales meetings. Old clients had promises made to keep them from leaving. Some of the employees knew that corners were being cut but couldn't do anything about it – there just wasn't enough time.

Most days, no one would see Sean nor Tim. The employees liked the autonomy given but were always fearful of being the one who pulled the last straw on a client before they left. It was hard to make a decision on the task to perform at any given time or how to best carry it out. When asked, Sean nearly always instructed the employee to give white glove service. Tim, however, would direct employees to take the most cost-effective route. In any case, the employees felt like they were spinning plates on the end of sticks, running around each other to keep each one spinning and trying desperately not to be the last one that touched it.

When I first spoke with Sean, he thought that the problem was his employees. "They just couldn't execute", he said, "but I can't afford to hire better employees". He was even tempted to rehire an employee that had great certifications but had been previously let go because of an altercation on a client site. Sean rehired the employee and let him work with clients remotely under a different name!

Sean was a smart man, and his business had a lot of potential. His big mistake was when his company started to catch on. He had hired a couple of good employees and brought on Tim at a great cost – a percentage of his company. It made sense to put someone in charge of the part of the business he liked the least, but he found that he lost control of his business.

Even though Sean had brought on some smart people, he didn't have the foundation – the frameworks – of the business that he wanted for the future. He didn't have the business models in place for Tim to carry out and nothing to measure that against. His employees didn't have a playbook to go by so that they could offer consistent service. Sean didn't have a community of other business leaders to help him make those decisions. Even though Tim could sell to enough clients, his business machine wasn't calibrated for growth and scale.

What you will get out of this book

Many times, a business owner will start a business and then in about five years start to wonder what sort of fever they must have had to sign up for such a large headache. Their business is in utter chaos, and they aren't finding the investment or the experience that they were looking for. Nights become restless, families are at odds with the business, the rich and famous lifestyle you thought you would have now seems like a wandering mirage.

The frameworks described in this book are just some of the fundamental models that a business needs to flourish. There are many other models and exercises that may more specifically help your business become more successful, but

Frameworks Consortium will provide a solid foundation for management and growth. This will help you understand what your business needs to run better right now and what you will need in the coming years, giving you the guiding principles to add to these frameworks.

This book will help you cultivate a mindset of thinking like an enterprise CEO. Through the pages of this book, readers will gain the insights needed to make key business decisions, find success in their initiatives, and develop a mindset that is focused on the long-term. Drawing from tried-and-true business concepts, this book offers comprehensive advice and guidance developed from some of the best minds in business. With these tools, readers can shape their thinking for optimal progress and profitability no matter what industry or niche they are targeting.

My personal mission is to help business owners love their business again. If you find valuable insight within these pages and make the commitment to carry them out, you will either love your business as you always wanted, or you will love your trip to the bank to cash the large check someone gave for your now valuable business.

George Mayfield

*"The fastest path to success starts with
knowing what your weaknesses are
and staring hard at them."*

— Ray Dalio

Where You Are Now

A successful journey has a specific destination and the best route to get there figured out before leaving. You must take an honest and precise look at where you are and the resources you have available before you can do either of those. Knowing where you are in business and mapping out the landscape of your current situation is essential to being able to develop effective and actionable strategies. It is difficult to know what risks and opportunities exist and what direction to plan without an understanding of where your business stands. Face the reality of your current state - be honest with yourself and don't shy away from assessing both the positive and negative elements of your venture. Once you understand where you are, only then can you think strategically about how you want to move forward.

The three common mistakes some make when looking at the current standing of their company are being dishonest with themselves, having an arrogant view of their competency, and an inaccurate perception of value. Ray Dalio, founder of Bridgewater Associates, has written "The fastest path to success starts with knowing what your weaknesses are and staring hard at them". It's imperative that you be honest with yourself as we begin by looking at where your business currently is. Honesty with oneself is essential for successful business planning. Without it, you cannot effectively assess the strengths and weaknesses of your strategy and adjust as needed.

Much like you need a true understanding of the market to make astute decisions on what direction your business should move in, you need an accurate self-assessment to create long-term success for yourself and your organization. It is important to be honest with yourself so that you can identify not only the potential benefits but also any risks associated with each decision. Taking honest inventory of where you currently stand - both professionally and personally - makes developing thoughtful strategies more achievable while also helping you build a foundation of trust between yourself and your companions.

Make sure that you rule out any delusions of competency before planning out your business strategies. This means that you should never assume that you are fully capable of making the best decisions without first doing the appropriate research and learning more about the current market and competitors. Taking shortcuts without properly understanding your circumstances can be extremely detrimental to your company's goals. Understanding your competitive landscape and customer needs is part of developing a sound business strategy and is essential for success. Doing your due diligence will not only help you to identify potential pitfalls, but also allow you to find opportunities that may prove beneficial to achieving your objectives.

It is important to understand the value of each step before you make any move in business. It can be tempting to skim corners and take shortcuts in an effort to cut costs, but these short-term savings often come at a higher cost in the long run. Having an inaccurate perception of value when planning your strategies can lead to efficiencies going untapped and result in lackluster results due to incorrect market assumptions or unanticipated complications. The best way to plan a course for success is to take the time for proper research and thought about the value of each decision, instead of going with what seems cheapest or easiest on the surface.

Your company machine

Seth and Darrin were two owners of Cozy Cottage Flooring, a company that specialized in flooring for high-end rural homes. They were proud of what they had accomplished. It had been six and a half years since they started the business, and they had built it up from nothing. They were both very good at flooring installations and knew everything there was to know about not only the surface material, but other materials that laid under the flooring and kept it lasting for years in the harshest of environments.

It seemed that every installation they did led to several referrals, and people paid them very good money to have a Cozy Cottage floor. Their business had grown so quickly that they were now hiring employees and opening a second location. However, the company had never really developed good business systems. The two owners did everything themselves and it was starting to take its toll. They were overworked and it was beginning to show in their service. Requests were going unanswered, employees had to be babysat on every job, several jobs had to be redone, and many jobs were half finished because product never arrived or would be sent to the wrong addresses. The tasks that relied on Seth and Darrin were just too much for them to keep track of as they had before. Not only was the business suffering, but the company's reputation was also suffering as a result.

What systems they did have didn't work together well and the business was breaking down. The two owners knew that they needed to fix things, but they didn't know how. They were at a loss as to what to do. They had never encountered this problem before, and they didn't know how to solve it. All they could do was watch as their business slowly fell apart.

***

Every company has a set of systems, processes, tools, and people that work together to convert resources into value for your clients and stakeholders. This has famously been referred to as a Value Chain and was coined by Michael Porter in his 1985 book "Competitive Advantage: Creating and Sustaining Superior Performance". It can be viewed as the schematics for the machine that is your business.

A set of primary activities help you to move products (or services) into and out of your company. The most obvious example would be a factory. It brings in parts or raw materials, puts them together into a finished good, then moves it out to a store or direct to users. Sales and Marketing help ensure that the product is needed and used. Service functions assist the customer after the purchase. Most of the time, these activities involve expenses that live in the cost of goods sold.

Another set of activities support your main business functions. Your company likely uses technologies like email, phone, and file storage among others. Human resources help you manage employee training, benefits, and hiring and firing. Your company may also develop new technologies and new ways to make your company more efficient. Procurement of goods and services your company uses is also a support activity. All these things help your company run and stay productive if they are working together.

You can get very deep into a Value Chain Analysis, and it may be appropriate to do so in some cases, especially if your marketing or overall business strategy really needs some work. In my experience, a higher-level view is enough for most mid-market businesses, at least to quickstart your understanding of the gaps in your business. As we continue to work through this book, we will discover the main parts of your company machine. We are going to make sure that all the parts of your machine are in working order, well oiled, and making effective contact with the other parts of your machine.

FIRM INFRASTRUCTURE
(e.g., Financing, Planning, Investor Relations)

HUMAN RESOURCE MANAGEMENT
(e.g., Recruiting, Training, Compensation System)

TECHNOLOGY DEVELOPMENT
(e.g., Product Design, Process Design, Market Research)

PROCUREMENT
(e.g., Services, Machines, Advertising, Data)

INBOUND LOGISTICS	OPERATIONS	OUTBOUND LOGISTICS	MARKETING & SALES	AFTER-SALES SERVICE
(e.g., Customer Access, Data Collection, Incoming Material Storage Service)	(e.g., Branch Operations, Assembly, Component Fabrication)	(e.g., Order Processing, Warehousing, Report Preparation)	(e.g., Sales Force, Promotion, Advertising, Proposal Writing, Website)	(e.g., Installation, Customer Support, Complaint Resolution, Repair)

PRIMARY ACTIVITIES

SUPPORT ACTIVITIES

MARGIN

VALUE
What buyers
are willing
to pay

Harvard Business School, 2022. https://www.isc.hbs.edu/strategy/business-strategy/Pages/the-value-chain.aspx

If you would like to know more about the Value Chain Analysis and how it can help your company achieve competitive advantage, I suggest reading "Understanding Michael Porter: The Essential Guide to Competition and Strategy" by Joan Magretta. It offers a concise view of Michael Porter's business theories and is good for those new to the subject or a refresher for those who studied it before.

Our organization, Frameworks Consortium, performs a Value Chain Analysis for all our new clients. You can find a link to reach out to us at the end of this book.

* * *

My father was the head engineer of a manufacturing plant that made attic and roof ventilation products. They had many machines that would take metal off rolls or sheets and stamp them into various parts. One would make an L shaped bracket with holes on both ends to mount a motor. Another might bend an entire flat square sheet into a dome with a rolled edge, while still cutting off the excess metal from the corners. Another long machine would take a coil of metal and, over the course of several yards of cutting wheels, turn that coil of metal into sections of screens.

One of his responsibilities was to run the machine shop, a team of people that oversaw all those cutting and shaping bits (called dies) as well as the operation of the machines. Whenever there was a problem, the machinist would first look at the manufactured parts. They would take a sample to the machine shop and use various tools to measure and compare against known good parts or master parts. This would tell the machinist not only that the machine was out of calibration but where to look at the machine first.

He would then watch the operator run the machine for a few minutes. He would watch how the metal was placed into the machine, where and how the operator stood, and how the machine was activated. He would watch how the giant, heavy flywheel would turn and how the pneumatic brakes would grab it in order to create a quick downward motion. He would watch how the various parts of the die would cut into the metal and which cuts were made first.

When any one of those moving parts were out of alignment, the quality of the produced parts would suffer, sometimes enough to warrant a shut down and recalibration.

In the same way, we need to look at how your business operates and what it produces. Your company machine takes various resources (such as raw materials, knowledge, and time) and converts them into a product or service that your customer values and is willing to pay you money for. The product isn't as good as it could be if your machine is out of calibration. If your machine runs bad enough, your customers will no longer see value in what it creates, and they will stop paying you for it.

Your company's machine is the foundational framework of your business. You need to know how it stands today and how you can continuously measure what it produces to know which part of the machine needs to be adjusted. The first step is to build a representation of your company value chain by looking at all the machine parts, the systems, people, and assets that your company uses. We'll call this your Machine Profile. Then, you must analyze the processes that move within and between each of those parts in your machine. The third step is to develop key performance indicators that will measure certain aspects of your company throughout the process.

Year after year, you will be able to compare how your business is running. By documenting and measuring each part of your company machine now, we establish a benchmark of how your company works. As we continuously track your company's performance, we will be able to tell how and if your machine is becoming more effective. You will know which parts are wearing out or which parts just don't fit as your company grows and changes.

Machine parts

If you've been in business very long, you know that you need two key financial documents to measure the productivity of your business, a balance sheet and an income statement. Just like a balance sheet is a snapshot in time for your business, your company's Machine Profile is a snapshot of your key systems and how they work together. Objectively examining and evaluating your Machine Profile can help you understand what makes your business different than your competitors and how you can benchmark your business to improve on itself.

Your company's Machine Profile is essentially a snapshot of all your key business systems with one goal in mind-to create value for yourself and your customers. While this may seem overly simplistic at first, there are many different factors that contribute to creating value in your business, from your finances and operations to marketing and customer experience. Typically, there are 5 major categories of your business that should be considered: Business Formation and Standing, Assets, Line of Business Software, 3rd Party Services, and Risk Aversion and Mitigation.

To get started with analyzing your company's Business Formation and Standing, we investigate how the business was set up and how it generally operates now. Was the business set up as an S-Corp, LLC, Sole proprietor? Are there other documented partnerships or shareholders? Is there a designated contact for billing? Emergencies? Customer support?

We also look at information about the company's reputation. What is the rating in Google Business? What is the public status of their tax filings? Have they claimed their Dunn and Bradstreet profile? What does a Whois lookup say about their domain?

Information like this allows you to discover areas in the setup of your company that may need some more looking into. Many times, a company is started without considering these items and some companies never fix these issues until they decide to sell the business. Later in this book, I will describe how you can use this public information to vet your service providers. You can bet that a lot of banks and lenders look at this information as well.

Cataloging your company's Assets is also an important part of understanding the health and productivity of your business. What are the fixed assets for the business? How are they used daily? Are they owned outright or on lease? How much debt financing do you have on them? What kind of depreciation schedules are used?

When you're getting started with evaluating your assets, it's important to have a good understanding of exactly what you have as well as the costs and potential risks associated with each asset. If your company owns vehicles, for example, you'll want to be certain you are keeping up with the required maintenance. If your company has in-house computer servers, you'll want to ensure they are secure and backed up regularly.

Even something as simple as a desk can be an asset, and it should be evaluated in the same way. Consider the amount of real estate your employees have to operate in. If there are employees who can't roll their chairs back without getting into another's space or tons of empty, unused space, you may want to consider real estate usage as a gap.

Your company's Line of Business Software is also a key part of your business's machine profile. This includes any software used for the day-to-day operations of your company, such as your accounting software or internal email system. It's important to evaluate your software regularly, especially if it is a custom system built just for your business needs. You'll want to look at things like the technology used, security and reliability of the software, how up to date it is with industry standards, cost of updates/maintenance, and how long the software has been in use.

Be sure to look at the line items in your books to see if you're still paying for software that is going unused or if there are multiple software that perform the same functions. Ask employees if there is "free" software that they use regularly. You may want to consider paying for business-grade resources that come with support and security agreements.

When it comes to evaluating your business's Machine Profile, you'll also want to look at your company's 3rd Party Services. These are any services that you use outside of the core operations of your business, such as bookkeepers, payroll services, or marketing firms. You'll want to evaluate these services in terms of how well they are integrated with your business and what their reputation is among your customers. Additionally, you'll want to make sure that the company is legally qualified and current on their licensing and registration, as well as any internal or external audits they may have.

Overall, when evaluating your company's Machine Profile, it's important to consider all the different areas that make up your business and how they interact with one another. By understanding your company's Machine, you can be better prepared to grow and adapt in the future and ensure that you're operating with maximum efficiency.

When you first built your balance sheet, you likely saw a few immediate problems. For example, the balances may have been off, the classifications might have been incorrect, and there may have been errors in the underlying data. When you first build the model of your company machine, you will see that there are parts that are not calibrated to work as well as they should. You may also see that there are parts missing entirely. These are gaps in your company that should be addressed. But don't panic or go into crisis mode now!

Remember that building a well-working machine takes time and should be done methodically. We still have a few more chapters to go before we start considering how to fill those gaps.

Processes

Now that you've documented the various parts of your company Machine, it important to understand how they all move together to create value for your customers. What puts these parts into motion is processes. Whether automatic, software-based processes or people-driven processes, you must understand where all those machine parts are and how they interact. You can more easily identify problems as they arise and take steps to rectify them by understanding the linkage between different aspects of your business. For example, if you notice that your sales are declining, it could be a sign that there's a problem somewhere in Marketing or perhaps the ball is getting dropped between Sales and Delivery. You can more easily prioritize which problems to tackle first and optimize your business machine for maximum efficiency by understanding the processes in your business.

So how do you get started? One of the easiest ways to assess the processes in your business is by using a process map. A process map is created by placing all your systems and sub-systems on a flowchart and drawing lines between them that illustrate how they interact with each other. This gives you a more visual representation of how your business operates and makes it easier to identify what processes you have in your business.

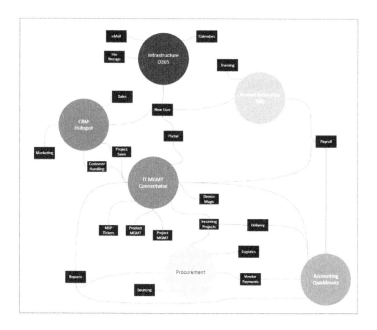

Frameworks Consulting, 2022

Identifying processes will help you understand how the different parts of your business interact and identify inefficiencies. For example, if you notice that the sales process is taking too long to get from prospect to customer, you can start looking for ways to streamline it. Maybe it's as simple as eliminating unnecessary steps or assigning someone internally to deal with certain tasks. However, if the problem is more complex, then you may need to investigate hiring additional staff or even outsourcing some of your sales process.

You may find that you have some processes that are overly complex. This may be because you have the wrong system or sub-system in place. You may discover that a part of your system seems to be broken. Problems in your processes should be documented as a potential gap that you'll need to prioritize and work on. It's ok to start to think of solutions for these process issues.

But don't run out the door and stop the Machine just yet!

Be sure to document each idea with enough detail to come back to later. You wouldn't want to put new processes in place just to confuse the team when you change them again. You'll have a better idea how to work on your systems and processes once you analyze all three parts of your machine.

* * *

John was a new operations manager of a small company who had struggled to find success. Under pressures from the owner, he was tasked with making improvements. He was expected to push for a quick turnaround.

Seeing that the sales had been dwindling, he started by switching out their Customer Relationship Management platform, believing that this would be the answer to all their problems. However, after several months of trying to get everyone on board with using it properly, they were still struggling with implementation and productivity loss. Undeterred, John continued looking for another solution – this time an Enterprise Resource Planning system – but again they ran into similar issues implementing it effectively and quickly gave up on it too.

Frustrated at yet another failed attempt at bringing success to the company, John kept searching for something better than what he already had implemented—regardless of the cost or disruption caused by constantly changing systems each time. But no matter what he tried nothing seemed to work; either because people weren't given enough training or because there wasn't enough thought put into how best use them within their organization's needs.

The team quickly grew tired of his constant changes and uncertainty; they were unable to plan ahead or stay focused as every month brought a different set of tools and processes with which they had to grapple. Meanwhile, John was in over his head and the owner seemed oblivious to their distress, driven by some higher purpose that only he could comprehend.

Finally, the company decided to bring in a consultant. John wasn't very happy about that, but he begrudgingly helped the consultant gather information on the people, processes, and systems they were using. John would complain to the owner that the consultant was a waste of money and time. He was still in the middle of implementing some new changes to the company's billing system and the consultant had advised against making any changes at all! Further, John would complain that ever since the consultant was hired, nothing has been made any better.

It took about two and a half months, but the consultant finally called for a meeting with the owner, John, and several other key employees. The consultant presented what he had found. The company's processes and systems looked like a rat's nest and nearly none of the departments were able to work together well. Data was lost in translation and there were numerous instances of the ball getting dropped on customer requests, many of whom left for a competitor.

45

The proposed solution was to re-identify the key systems and make sure that they were using the best solutions for that company's industry and size. It would mean that several systems they already had would go unused -- a wasted sunk cost. It also meant that there would be several manhours of cleaning up data and making records consistent. In some cases, it made sense to scrap the data and start completely fresh, entering all customer transactions from that point on as "new records".

John fumed. It sounded to him like it was 10 steps backwards! The owner approved the project, nevertheless. It took just over another year to finally get all the systems in place as they needed to be, but each month leading to that were small improvements. Each subsequent improvement seemed to have more and more impact on the company's production, though. The next year, the company was back on track and highly competitive with their local rivals.

John, unfortunately, never caught on. After several months of pushing and almost sabotaging the projects, he found the opportunity to pursue other interests. He went on to tell all his friends that he quit because the owners wanted to implement something "stupid", and it seemed like a waste of time. Little did he know what had been implemented turned out to be the saving grace of the company.

This is a classic example of why implementing solutions without adequate planning can not only be costly but can also be detrimental to a company's growth and success. As the leader of an organization, it is important that you take a holistic view when evaluating solutions to problems. It's not just about finding the cheapest or fastest solution - it's about making sure that all aspects of the organization are considered and work together.

Understanding the processes in your business is critical to optimizing your machine and ensuring that it's running at peak efficiency. With a clear understanding of how all the different parts of your company work together, you'll be better equipped to make smart decisions that help you grow and thrive in an increasingly competitive market.

Key performance indicators

When viewed holistically, your company's key performance indicators (KPIs) are like an income statement. It is a report card of how your company is functioning. You can see trends over the duration of time that help you to understand how your company is improving or if it is not improving as expected when taking these measurements consistently. Certain key performance indicators can be compared to other KPIs to better understand how systems are functioning together. Monitoring your KPIs can give you a high-level view of how various areas of your business are performing, which can help you identify opportunities for improvement.

Consider you are driving in your car. The dashboard in front of you shows you several KPIs. Speed, mileage, oil temperature, even the clock gives you information about your drive. It's telling you how your car is operating and providing data to help you make decisions on reaching your destination. There are other KPIs that may not always be on your dashboard. Tire pressure, miles since your last oil change, average MPG. These KPIs may not matter to you as often or may only matter when there's a problem. Nevertheless, they are still measuring your progress and allowing you to act if need be. Just like in driving, KPIs tell you how your business is operating and can help you make decisions to best reach your business goals.

One of the most important aspects of using key performance indicators is to be consistent with your measurements. This means taking measurements at regular intervals and comparing them to previous measurements to see how your company is doing. This allows you to better understand how your company is improving or not improving. If you only take measurements once, you may not get an accurate picture of how your company is performing. By taking measurements consistently, you can identify trends and make changes accordingly.

Not only should you measure KPIs consistently, but you must monitor them consistently as well. Going for periods of time without reviewing your company's performance can lead to blind spots that affect your ability to make well-informed decisions. As an example, you could find yourself in a bit of trouble if you aren't consistently checking your speed against the posted speed limit as you drive down the road. It's too late to do anything about it as you see the lights flashing in your rear-view mirror. Similarly, you may get stuck with costly errors or problems in your business if you are not regularly reviewing your key performance indicators. If your KPIs are consistently being monitored, you can identify potential issues sooner, which gives you more time to take action.

This isn't to say that all KPIs should be reviewed at the same intervals. Some KPIs should be reviewed weekly, such as production levels for a factory or customer reviews for a restaurant. Others should be reviewed monthly or quarterly, including financial reports, employee hours saved through automation, and customer retention. Also, certain KPIs should be reviewed annually or biennially. For example, a company's long-term debt may only be reassessed every year or two. Just like KPIs in your car, don't try to watch everything all the time. There's a difference between managing by KPIs and micromanaging by KPIs.

If you stared at your car's dashboard while driving or tried to watch all the information about your car at once, you'd surely wreck. Your business is no different. KPIs need to be watched, but there's an appropriate timeliness for each one.

Another important aspect of KPIs is comparing them to your target performance levels. Each of your KPIs should have a target or target range. That means that there's either a goal to hit, ie: 5 new client sales per week, or a range to fall between, ie: Less than 18 and higher than 10 new service requests per week. Less than 10 service requests may mean that people don't find your service desk easy to use, while more than 18 means that there may be a quality control issue.

It's ok to not know what the target should be at first. Use your gut feeling and put a number out there. You can move it to a more realistic number as you begin collecting data.

You can get a clearer picture of how well your company is performing by comparing some of your KPIs to others. Sometimes a rise in one KPI can be explained by the rise in another, or perhaps it's the inverse. Back to your car, it's obvious that your oil temperature would be low if the external thermometer was also low. A blatantly astute observation, but it does illustrate how two KPIs could be equally important and measured separately, but still related by causation. Correlation doesn't always mean that there's causation, but it takes a critical mind to analyze your KPIs as a whole.

Each KPI is measuring different systems and processes in your company and can't all be treated in the same way. Just like an engineer looking at a machine's output, you need to understand that each KPI has different tolerances. A 10% difference in daily production may be a non-issue, but a 10% difference in sales calls made could be a problem. A good practice is to discuss with your managers what the acceptable tolerances are when the KPI is created. Then, you'll have a red line to know when a KPI needs to trigger a discussion or deeper analysis. Tolerance can always be changed, but it shouldn't be changed often.

Be ready to act when a KPI is telling you that there may be an issue. The beauty of KPIs is that they can tell you when something is not right and allow you to address the issue before it becomes a bigger problem. However, if you just sit back and hope that the problem fixes itself, you may end up having bigger issues to deal with. When a KPI is telling you that something might be wrong, invest the time and resources to determine what's happening so that you can act on it before the problem gets any worse.

You're likely to find even more gaps as you and your team develop a set of well-rounded KPIs that give a big picture view of your company's performance. During the onboarding process for our clients, we implement a set of at least 15 KPIs that monitor the company from the perspective of 5 business disciplines. It is not uncommon that we find it impossible to accurately calculate one or more KPIs. Sometimes the business just doesn't have a system in place to gather data.

***

I was working with a really interesting client that sold a very special part for the construction of highways. There were very few competitors, and he was well known in the regional industry. As we were walking his company through the process of documenting how our KPIs were to be gathered, we found that he didn't use a Customer Relationship Management tool. He only worked through email since he started his company almost 8 years prior. Things seemed to work out fine, so he never thought much of it. Vendors would put in an order, and it would get processed.

The problem identified itself as we began to work on tracking sales conversion time, the time it took from a salesperson to generate a lead to converting that lead into a client. This was important because the owner, Eric, established that his 3-year goal was to expand his reach into other regions. He had hired a few salespeople that would be starting that next month and wanted to make sure that the salespeople were performing, especially since they would be out on the road and out of sight for the most part.

"Well, how are we tracking sales conversion time right now?" I had asked.

51

He wasn't. He had hired a few people here and there to help him with sales, but they were mostly just helping prepare the orders. No one had even thought that there would be a tool to track sales. Before our talks, Eric was simply going to pay them based on the amount of sales dollars that came in.

"How are you going to attribute the time one person spends on a potential client if they take longer to become a client. How will you know if too much time is being spent per client? If we aren't looking at the sales process from start to finish for each salesperson, how will you identify problems in the process? The next states we're going to be working in may not be like this one, and you've been here awhile."

Eric pursed his lips in thought. Even before he opened his company, he had close ties with people in the civil construction industry.

I gave him a few seconds to let that settle in and told him. "Eric, if we don't have a sales tool in place and we only go by revenue, the sales function is only a Go/No Go decision. You may end up firing good salespeople or keeping ones that know how to fake the system".

We ended up assisting Eric with a vendor that brought in a CRM and provided training for this new tool. Not only did it help Eric know what was going on at each step of the sales process and by whom, it helped gain more customers in his home region by giving him the ability to send out drip campaigns and re-order reminders.

Let's look at a few examples of KPIs that we typically look at with our clients and what they show our C-Suite consultants. We look at these KPIs on a monthly basis so that we can help guide the business and watch for problematic trends. We can propose a discussion with the client when the KPIs point to issues. That discussion may give us a point of reference, or we may need to perform a deep dive to investigate the company in greater detail.

Along with these KPIs, we encourage businesses to break some of these KPIs into team and weekly indicators so that they have better visibility into what might cause changes in the KPIs, either departmentally, or by person. The addition of some other industry or business specific indicators can prove to be helpful as well.

Keep in mind that these KPIs are just some of the examples our C-Suite looks at and that these are meant to be wide-view snapshots of that measurement. They may not account for every detail in the function that it's measuring, but that's where the team weekly KPIs come in.

Average Cost Per Full Time Employee - This number includes a total of employee benefits, payroll, payroll management systems, taxes, training systems, and recruiting expenses. Dividing this number by the number of employees for that month and you have your KPI. You may need to also take an average number of employees for that month if you have higher turnover.

(Average Cost Per Full Time Employee)
= (Total Costs of employees) / (Number
or avg of Employees)

It's important to allocate an appropriate number of resources for employee compensation. Being too stingy with spending isn't ideal, yet there are measures that can be taken to increase the efficiency and cost-effectiveness of your company's management expenses - all while ensuring improved benefits for employees. Monitoring these values is paramount as any sudden changes could indicate other underlying issues within the business organization during a period of scaling up operations.

The amount invested in employees will differ from business to business; the employment tactic should mirror the company's Mission, Values, and Culture. Your overhead costs can either be an invaluable asset or a particularly costly burden, depending on the services and business goals in question. Investing in the right human capital to bring your organization's visions to life is essential for lasting success.

What would trigger a deep dive?
- Drastic, unexplained fluctuations
- Low number with Low Workforce Maturity
- High number with High Workforce Maturity
- High number with low Talent Satisfaction

What would a deep dive look for?
- High employment advertising costs
- High management costs
- Retention Rate
- Turnover Rate
- Training Programs/Processes
- HR Management Processes
- Cost per Hire

Average Throughput - This KPI is a bit tailored to the company's main process, whether that is a consultant, plumber, or retailer. The inventory is the value that is provided to their customer. For a CPA firm, that may be accounts processed per day. For plumbers, that may be jobs per day. For Consultants, that might be meetings per day or consulting hours worked per day. Retail and manufacturing could be a bit more obvious. These are averaged out for the month. Time is simply the number of days your company had available to work that month, usually 20-21 days or 21.62 on average.

(Average Throughput) = (Inventory) /
(Work Days)

Understanding the concept of flow rate is a pivotal step to making informed decisions regarding everything from investment to production and, ultimately, revenue. Subsequently, knowing what numbers (and the processes that create them) are considered to measure throughput rate could potentially have a profound effect on increasing profits for your business. Ultimately, leveraging this information can help you make smart choices that may positively influence company finances in both short-term and long-term ways.

The throughput rate should be somewhat consistent with market benchmarks and should rise or lower given expectations in the market. This can be determined by comparing your company's numbers with market averages and considering external factors, such as competition or changes in production costs. You should expect to see higher numbers if you are mature in your market or have special processes that your competitors do not.

Conversely, you should expect to see lower output if you are new in the market or have the same processes as everyone else. That doesn't make either number necessarily "good" or "bad".

Remember that industry and market is not the same thing. Consider two companies: Little Cesar's Pizza and the high-end pizza restaurant in your neighborhood. These two companies are in the same industry, but not in the same market. Little Cesar's should expect to see higher output since their market is those wanting quick and cheap pizza. Your high-end pizza restaurant sells quality pizza and a great experience. Make sure you benchmark appropriately.

What would trigger a deep dive?
- Sudden drops in production
- Steady declines
- Poor rate given market benchmarks

What would a deep dive look for?
- Bad or no Processes
- Employee turnover
- Market Forces
- Leadership Issues

Mean Time Between Failures - The Mean Time Between Failures, or MTBF, evaluates the average duration of system malfunctions until resolution. We look at this number for a client's technical stack. We can determine a system failure rate by analyzing large-scale components such as general crashes, VoIP disconnections, and network availability. MTBF is the total number of operational days divided by the number of failures for each month.

(Mean Time Between Failures) =
(Operational Days) / (Number of
Failures)

IT dependability is an essential characteristic of any operation. Businesses ought to assess the probability of availability for their IT systems and attempt to anticipate malfunctions. This figure will indicate when it's time to substitute, reconfigure, or modify processes/training related with IT systems. The longer the MTBF for a system, the more reliable it is likely to be before faltering. If numbers are declining, this could potentially signal an unresolved issue with your system.

What would trigger a deep dive?
-   Sudden low numbers
-   Lowering numbers over time

What would a deep dive look for?
-   RCA (Root Cause Analysis) history
-   Organizational changes
-   Process Changes
-   Age of equipment
-   Security breaches

Current Ratio - The current ratio is a key metric used to measure the liquidity of a business. It is calculated by dividing the total current assets of a company by its total current liabilities. The higher the ratio, the more liquid and better able to cover short-term obligations the company is considered to be. A low current ratio can indicate that a company may not have enough cash or other resources available to pay off its short-term debts when they come due. For this reason, it's important for businesses to keep

57

an eye on their current ratios and ensure that they remain within an acceptable range.

$$(Current\ Ratio) = (Current\ Assets) / (Current\ Liabilities)$$

The Current Ratio is an indicator of a business's financial wellness. Comparisons between businesses in different industries may be of limited utility; however, contrasting against the previous months and related enterprises will likely yield more beneficial results.

For most companies, a ratio between 1.5 and 3 is optimal. Depending on how established the company has become or which industry it belongs to, certain aspects must be taken into consideration when calculating its current ratios. Industries often require differing operational models, procedures within their business operations as well as cash flows which will affect these calculations accordingly.

What would trigger a deep dive?
- A ratio lower than 1 may indicate liquidity issues
- A ratio over 3 may mean that a company is not managing its capital properly
- Inconsistent changes in ratio

What would a deep dive look for?
- Incorrect calculation of ratio
- Inconsistent accounting practices
- Debts utilized properly

Revenue vs Sales Target – The Revenue vs Sales Target ratio is a calculation based on the increase in revenue against the revenue target set by the company. This means that if the revenue is equal to the sales target, then it would be '1'. The Revenue vs Sales Target ratio is generally used by companies as a tool to help assess and evaluate the performance of sales in their business. Revenue is a simple number to calculate, but your sales target should be a number that makes sense for your target market. There are several factors that can affect this ratio, including changes in market conditions, fluctuations in consumer spending behavior, and other external factors. Internal factors to consider would be the product you are offering, pricing strategies, and how it is being promoted and delivered to the customer.

(Revenue vs Sales Target) = ((Ending Revenue) – (Starting Revenue)) / (Sales Revenue Target)

A company should look at their revenue vs sales target in order to get a better understanding of the success of the business and how well they are meeting their sales goals. The ratio provides key insight into how the company is performing in terms of sales and can help them identify areas for improvement or where changes could be made to increase their bottom line. It is important for companies to closely monitor this ratio, as it can have a significant impact on their success.

If your sales team's performance is below the benchmark, or if their targets are too ambitious to reach, this could be a red flag. Unexpected and continuous shortfalls would indicate that further investigation may be necessary.

What would trigger a deep dive?
- Consistent underperforming sales

- Low or high targets compared to industry standards

What would a deep dive look for?
- Justification of sales targets
- Sales processes and training
- Sales team turnover

Key performance indicators are a vital tool for monitoring the health of your company and making informed decisions that will lead to growth and success. To be effective, you must take regular measurements, monitor them regularly, compare them to each other and your target performance levels, and act when necessary. By doing so, you can maximize the value of KPIs in your company and achieve your goals.

* * *

Your business is a Machine that converts resources into value for your customers. As a business leader, you are the technician for that machine. You must understand all its parts intimately, you must know how all the parts work together, and you must keep your eye on its production to know if it's working well.

A good business leader knows that they must invest in this machine as the company grows. The same machine you started the business with isn't the one that will make you break past a million in revenue, and that's not the same machine that will allow you to pass 10 or 50 million in revenue. If you try to keep scaling revenue without building on and improving your machine, you'll overwork yourself and your machine. It'll break down.

Some entrepreneurs see this as hard work (it is) and decide to limit revenue and stay small. Others want more. They know the only way to get more is to build a better machine. They're willing to put in the time and resources, accepting that it's going to take a while, because they're patient and know that eventually the machine will be so efficient that it can scale revenue much more quickly. It's not easy. It takes putting in the work on your business, and it takes planning.

George Mayfield

"When you make a business, you get to make a little universe where you control all the laws. This is your utopia."

— Derek Sivers, Anything You Want: 40 Lessons for a New Kind of Entrepreneur

Where You Want to Be

Where you want your company to be in the next 3 to 5 years should be something that is written down, communicated to your team, and referenced when making decisions. It all starts with a vision – that dream of what you want your company to be. That vision becomes reality through strategy, the plan that successfully puts your value machine to work in the way that it is most effective. Tactics, your strategy in practice, can quickly change when needed, but your Vision and Strategy should remain largely steadfast. What your company does and how it carries it out - its competitive strategy should be built on and improved over time.

***

Michelle owned an appliance repair company, Warranty Plus Total. Bored with her residential real estate business, she saw an opportunity as her clients would move into a new house and inherit the appliances that came with the home. She knew that Home Warranties were a huge pain and wanted to offer a done-for-you service that would work with the warranty companies she was so familiar with.

Her company was a success in a relatively short amount of time. Her knowledge of home warranties and steady customer base almost guaranteed success. She soon dropped out of the real estate business entirely and focused on the appliance business. She had a few employees that were excellent in appliance repair and another, Cassie, who Michelle had trained in dealing with home warranty companies. Cassie was the one who completed most of the paperwork and followed up with the claims. Warranty Plus Total was well known in the area as the company that would take care of all the headache of warranty claims. She kept costs down by operating in a low rent space in the industrial area of town and performing most of the repairs in the clients' homes.

A few years later, Michelle was at an appliance trade show where she saw many of the latest models that were coming out. She got excited to see the capabilities that they had, connecting to the internet to add items to shopping carts, sending alerts to the user when food was done, some could even play music off the user's playlist! "This is the future of appliances" she thought. She felt like her appliance repair revenue had leveled off and it was time to bring in new kinds of business. She called up her business coach and excitedly explained her idea.

The next week Michelle met with her banker and secured a loan for a retail space near several high-end furniture stores - the kind that have customers that would buy these new smart devices. The store was amazing with fancy lighting and plenty of showroom space. All of her employees were brought into that location as well since she could only afford to operate in one location after the business loan was taken out.

Some other changes were made, too. Now that they're in the high-end appliance industry, she had all her employees wearing uniforms, Nice Khaki slacks and a green logo embroidered polo. Cassie was one of her most loyal employees and had always been exceptionally good with customers over the phone, so Michelle reasoned that she would be a good salesperson, too.

It wasn't a year before Michelle realized what a mistake she had made. It became obvious looking back that Cassie must have begun her job search right when the move happened. The repair employees were either let go or were switched to not-so-great salespeople after the warranty business stopped coming in entirely. Michelle was stuck with a high rent location and too many employees who couldn't sell anything.

Michelle's mistake was that she didn't stick to her original vision. She had a good competitive advantage - her relationships and knowledge with home warranty companies. While her business coach was right in that she needed to change something to keep growing, she should not have abandoned what made her company so different. There would have been multiple other ways to scale her company while retaining the core competencies and unique resources that made it successful to begin with.

Vision

Whether you started your company, bought into it, or were hired for a leadership position, you likely had a vision of what you were going to do with the company. Maybe you had a picture in your head of the company working in multiple states or having its name and logo on a high-rise. Perhaps you dreamed of increasing the company's value and being able to compensate its employees much more than they were. Your vision for the company is important because it gives people a goal to move towards. But your vision should be more than just a lofty goal. You should also envision how your company's Machine will operate and how your company will continue to utilize its special sauce in an increasingly meaningful way.

Your company vision is made up of your core values, your mission, your long-term goals, and the niche market you intend to serve. And while it is important to be able to articulate these elements of your vision, it is also essential that you can put them into action. This means that your company should have a solid strategy for how to develop and maintain its Machine, as well as for how it will continue to differentiate itself from its competitors.

Your company's core values are the foundation of your culture. They define how you behave, what is important to you, and how you make decisions. Core values should be shared by everyone in the company and should be visible in everything you do. They should also be revisited on a regular basis to ensure that they still reflect the company's beliefs and goals. Some common core values include honesty, integrity, respect, and accountability. But you can choose whatever values resonate with your company and its employees. Just make sure that they are meaningful to your team and that they guide your actions.

Your company's mission is what it stands for and what it intends to do. It should be brief and easy to understand, and it should be something that you can communicate to your customers, employees, and investors. Your mission should also be something that you are passionate about and that inspires you to work hard. And it should be something that is achievable, so that people can see how your company is making a difference in the world.

Some companies choose to focus on social responsibility, while others focus on making a profit. Your mission statement should be inspirational, not only to you and your team but also to your customers. It is important that the message behind your company's mission can be conveyed easily and accurately.

A company's long-term goals are what it hopes to achieve in the future. They should be realistic and achievable, but they should also be ambitious enough to inspire employees and customers. Some common long-term goals include becoming a market leader, expanding into new markets, increasing profits, and developing new products or services. You can pick goals that fit with your company and its employees. See to it that they are essential to your team and that they spur you to do your best work.

Your company's strategy for achieving its long-term goals should be well thought out and achievable. It should also be something that you can explicitly communicate to your employees, customers, and investors. And it should be revisited on a regular basis to ensure that it still reflects the company's beliefs and goals.

One way to achieve your long-term goals is by setting S.M.A.R.T goals. S.M.A.R.T goals are specific, measurable, achievable, relevant, and time bound. This means that they are specific enough so that you can track progress, measurable so that you can determine whether or not you have achieved them, achievable so that they are within your reach, relevant to your company's mission and long-term goals, and time-bound so that you have a deadline for completing them.

S.M.A.R.T goal setting is an important part of effective planning, and it can help you stay focused and motivated as you work towards your company's vision.

Your company's core values, mission, and long-term goals should all be aligned with each other. This will help to ensure that everyone in the company is working towards the same goal, and it will also help to differentiate your company from its competitors.

Your competition is the other companies that are going after the same customers as you. That's why it's important to decide on your niche market. This is the group of people that your product or service is meant to serve. It could be a specific demographic, and it could also be an interest or a need. Once you know who your target market is, you can focus on meeting their needs and delivering value to them.

Just as your vision for the company was important, so is maintaining that vision. As you begin to grow, it can be easy to lose sight of what originally inspired you about this business and why you started it in the first place. It's critical to continually revisit your original calling and how that connects with your current priorities. place. This will help you to focus on what matters most and keep you moving in the right direction.

Strategy

If your vision is a theoretical picture of how your company will look in the future, your strategy is the actual plans to get it from where it is today to that vision. There is a big difference between creating a business strategy based on proven business theories and just a couple of people in a room throwing ideas at the wall.

Your strategy should be your written guide for how you and your team will carry out your vision. It doesn't have to be detailed. As a matter of fact, it should be high level enough to be flexible and allow your team to work within its guidelines.

But how do you even get started in thinking about what the best things for your company to do are? It helps to start by developing a SWOT analysis.

A swot analysis is oftentimes disregarded. It's taught to many as early as grade school and usually covered in business management 101. It's an easy concept to grasp, so its value is underestimated. However, a SWOT is a powerful tool.

A brief overview of SWOT - A SWOT considers strengths, weaknesses, opportunities, and threats, usually in a block diagram. At its core, a SWOT analysis is a tool that can be used to help businesses identify areas where they excel and where they may need improvement. It can be particularly useful when it comes to planning strategy or making decisions about the future.

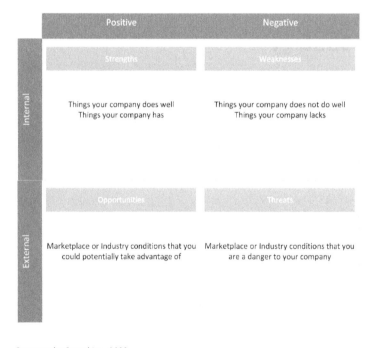

Frameworks Consulting, 2022

Strengths and weaknesses are internal to your company. Simply, what does your company currently have or does that is a good thing, and what does your company do poorly or lack. Put your blinders on and look inwards only.

A strength might be that you have highly skilled employees, patents, or a lot of capital. It could be unique processes or proprietary assets. It could even be relationships with vendors. Keep in mind that the more unique a strength is, the more power it gives your company. Despite the fact that your competitors all have this strength, it should not be overlooked or discounted. If there is something within your company that helps it do what it does, write it down. If you end up sharing too many strengths with your competitors, you will likely have a strategic problem.

A weakness might be that your company is young, struggles with cash flow, or lacks recognizable branding. You may have poor relations with your vendors or lack any unique processes. Weaknesses can also be shared within your competitive market. Many of the time clients struggle with identifying weaknesses. It's difficult to look inward and be critical of ourselves. Some in the room might even get outright offended. It is advantageous to be straightforward and candid about any areas in which your business may not excel. Refer to some of the gaps that we've already discovered as those may be some of your biggest weaknesses.

Opportunities and Threats are external to your company. They consider the competitive environment your business operates in as well as macro-economic factors such as government policy, demographic movements, or shifts in cultural trends. These two factors together form the external environment of your business.

Some common opportunities that companies look for include changes in consumer tastes or technology, new markets, emerging markets that compliment your offering, new tax laws, or competitors exiting the market. To find new opportunities, you should keep an eye out for data that indicates that something has changed or is about to change. One of the key ways that companies can find new opportunities is by tracking changes in consumer tastes or technology. For example, if you notice that consumers are becoming more interested in buying sustainable products, this could be an opportunity to develop a new product line focused on environmentally friendly materials or manufacturing processes. Additionally, many businesses rely on emerging technologies such as AI or blockchain in order to automate processes, enhance product quality and performance, or improve the customer experience. While new opportunities can arise out of unexpected circumstances, it's often helpful to track changes in your industry so that you don't miss any potential opportunities.

Don't get caught up in the opportunities that present themselves to you. Oftentimes, I've witnessed clients become captivated and brimming with enthusiasm when they begin conceptualizing fresh business opportunities. The thrill of brainstorming can lead them to try to jump into action prior to properly planning for these prospects. Remember that this is just part of looking at your business as a whole. Jot the ideas down and move on.

Threats may be new compliance requirements, consumer law, or lack of talent in the employment pool. Government policies can significantly impact your company's operations, from new regulations that increase compliance requirements to shifts in tax laws that affect your bottom line. Additionally, demographic movements and cultural trends may influence customer preferences and purchasing behavior, which can also have a significant impact on your business performance. When analyzing the external environment, it is important to take a holistic approach. Rather than focusing on one factor or trend in isolation, look at how that factor relates to other aspects of your business. Consider what is going on globally – even if you do not operate outside of your city limits.

If you feel stumped, one good way to look at all the external factors of your organization is to use a PESTEL analysis. PESTEL is a popular strategic business exercise that examines the external factors impacting an organization. It stands for Political, Economic, Social, Technological, Environmental, and Legal. It is used to identify the major opportunities and threats of an organization in order to develop a comprehensive strategy for success.

The Political Factor focuses on national and local government policies and regulations that can impact the organization. For example, changes in tax or immigration laws may make it more difficult to recruit and retain employees, which could negatively affect an organization's profitability.

The Economic Factor addresses trends such as GDP growth rates and inflation rates, both of which can impact a business' ability to expand or achieve profitability. For example, a recession may slow the growth of demand for an organization's products or services and make it more difficult to hire talented employees with competitive salaries.

The Social Factor focuses on consumer preferences, which can drive changes in the demand for organizations' products or services. For example, if a growing number of consumers prefer products that are sustainably or ethically produced, an organization may need to change its production methods in order to meet this demand and remain competitive.

The Technological Factor targets the ever-changing nature of technology, which can drive new innovations or increased competition. For example, digitization and automation have driven changes in the marketplace, and some organizations may find themselves disrupted by more technologically savvy rivals.

The Environmental Factor focuses on environmental concerns, such as climate change, water scarcity, and air pollution. For example, an organization's production processes may need to be redesigned to take these factors into account.

The Legal Factor of PESTEL concentrates on national and local laws that may impact an organization's operations. This includes things like labor laws, health and safety regulations, intellectual property rights, antitrust regulations, and consumer protection laws. It is important for organizations to be aware of these legal requirements in order to remain compliant with the law and avoid any potential penalties or fines. Additionally, understanding the legal environment can also help organizations identify opportunities for growth or expansion by taking advantage of favorable legislation or tax incentives. By staying up to date on changes in the legal landscape, organizations can ensure they are well positioned to succeed in a dynamic business environment.

PESTEL Analysis is a powerful strategic business tool that enables organizations to identify the major opportunities and threats they face. By examining these key areas in detail, organizations can gain valuable insights into their current situation and develop strategies to achieve continued success.

Another thing to note about a SWOT analysis is that something that is an internal strength may also be a weakness. Perhaps all your employees have been working for you for a long while. While it is great to have experience and loyalty on your team, this familiarity can breed complacency or cause your ideas to become stale. These are both two sides of the same coin. Likewise, an external opportunity can also be a threat. Maybe your main vendor is overseas and economic factors have caused their prices to be much lower. This could be a great opportunity to load up on your inventory. It's also possible that this causes a threat to your company because the low prices may allow more competitors to join the market. So, it's crucial to take a comprehensive look at your internal and external factors when performing a SWOT analysis.

Take as much time as you need on your SWOT. Take some time to think about it over the weekend and get input from your team members and contacts. Hours after a SWOT analysis session, it's not unheard of for people to keep ruminating on the strengths, weaknesses, opportunities, and threats they discussed. As the day winds down, you may be surprised to discover some of your most profound revelations.

Once your SWOT is generated, you can begin to pair the items in each area together. Look at your strengths and find the ones that can be paired with opportunities. Can one or more of your strengths help you find success in an opportunity? Are any of those strengths that may be unique to your business? This is a great place to start when you're planning for growth. By examining the opportunities and seeing which of your strengths can be paired with them, your business can grow faster by leveraging what you already do well. An example of this might be a small business bank that has a great relationship with their customers (strength). They may have an opportunity to grow by expanding into different locations if they see that their customers have begun to move into other areas of the state (opportunity), and they have the capital (strength) to build in those new locations.

Compare the internal weaknesses that you have with the external threats of your market. Will any of your weaknesses be compounded by a threat? Is there any way to mitigate that risk? This can help you decide which weaknesses to focus on when planning your business strategy. Your company may be relatively new in the market (weakness), and you see that the threat of new entrants to the market is high (threat). Combine that with the added weakness that your marketing budget is low and you may find that this is something that your business will want to watch for and plan against. Find some way to outmaneuver any new competitors and gain market share as quickly as possible from more mature competitors.

Cross examine and you may find that a threat can be countered by one of your strengths. Perhaps you see that your competitors are offering a product or service at a lower cost than you and your business is going to have to adjust as a result. Look for ways you can leverage what makes your company unique (strength) to counteract the threat. Perhaps you have a long-standing relationship with one of the suppliers that you can use to negotiate better pricing or work jointly to reduce costs. If you are able to overcome the threat, your business can continue growing and succeeding.

Lastly, you may realize that a potential opportunity could be lost due to one of your weaknesses. While this may seem counterproductive, it's important to consider that if your competitors do not share that weakness, they may be able to take advantage of that opportunity. This is where you must decide if that opportunity outweighs the risk of any potential loss. Let's say that the government passes a new bill for funding research and development. If your company is one of the few small businesses able to take advantage of that opportunity, then you may want to invest in R&D spending as a result. However, if your company does not have much experience with this type of research or that area isn't where you are best at, it will probably be more difficult for you to succeed in that field. You may want to pass on the opportunity and instead focus on new strengths or areas where your company is more successful.

Consider these in your company strategy and how they will help or hurt you when carrying out your vision. If you feel up to it, you may even expand on that and assume that your competitors are doing the same analysis. Take your closest three

George Mayfield

competitors and do your best to perform a SWOT analysis for them. Doing so might give you a great advantage in seeing what they may be doing and why, even if it's different than your own.

Apart from a SWOT, there are other strategic business exercises that businesses can use to assess their internal and external environments. These include the Boston Consulting Group's Market Position Analysis, or MPA (which is based on relative market share analysis and environmental trends or forces), Porter's Five Forces analysis (which seeks to uncover how industry forces of competition, buyers, suppliers, potential entrants and substitutes impact a business), PIMS analysis (clients are divided into value-added segments according to growth rate rather than sales volume) and McKinsey 7-S framework as suggested by Tom Peters in his book "In Search of Excellence".

Each of these strategic business exercises has its own strengths and weaknesses. The MPA, for example, is an effective way to get a quick snapshot view of how one's company compares with its competitors in terms of market share and the external forces that are impacting it. However, it does not provide specific information on what levers can be used to improve performance or increase competitiveness over time. Similarly, Porter's Five Forces analysis provides valuable insights into each industry force but may not be as relevant when applied across different industries due to differences in competitive dynamics. Likewise, PIMS analysis requires segmentation data by value-added segments (such as low/medium/high growth) which may be difficult for some businesses to access. Finally, McKinsey's 7-S framework helps companies identify their strategy and structure but is based on

78

the assumption that strategic issues occur at the level of the entire organization, which may not be relevant for some companies.

As with all strategic business exercises, the key to leveraging these tools effectively lies in identifying what is most relevant for your company and using it to gain actionable insights. In other words, the objective of a SWOT analysis or any other strategic business exercise is not just to understand where a company stands but also to identify areas for improvement and opportunities for growth. By focusing on identifying, measuring, and managing against key business objectives, you can leverage the relative strengths of each exercise to create a winning strategy for your company.

Now that you have a good idea of what to consider when developing your strategy, you can begin prioritizing actions that you need to take. Each one of these actions will need a list of initiatives, a priority score for each, and, unfortunately, a budget. In working with my clients, I have found that breaking the strategy into 6 parts helps in both developing and carrying out its actions.

***

Company Strategy - Your company strategy should be the first strategy worked through and will most likely take the longest. Your company strategy is most important because it will drive your departmental strategies. It needs to cover how your company plans to navigate the micro and macro environment, that is, how you will outperform and differentiate from your competitors and how you will take advantage of environmental, economic, and governmental opportunities.

Your company strategy should lead and guide your departmental strategies. While the company strategy is the overall marching order for the business, departmental strategies consider how each function of the business will carry out the mission within its discipline.

Make sure to let your previous analysis guide you as you prioritize activities. Don't let emotion and ego get in the way of your decision-making process. Your company strategy should be based on sound logic, and not just what you think sounds good. When thinking about your departmental strategies, make sure to consider how each is unique and individually fits into the larger scope of your overall business strategy.

* * *

Sales and Marketing Strategy - A good sales and marketing strategy is integral to the success of any business. It should be tailored to the specific company and its customers and should be fluid enough to adapt as the market changes. The key components of a successful sales and marketing strategy include market research, target markets, product positioning, pricing strategy, promotion, and sales tactics.

An effective marketing strategy requires having a clear plan for how to capture more market share. By doing so, businesses can gain greater profits, which can then be reinvested in any operational gaps that need to be addressed. Start by looking at your industry and examining what the existing competition is doing. Considering your company's unique machine, create a strategy that will differentiate your business from the competition. Continue to be proactive in staying ahead of trends and understanding how customer needs are evolving so you can make informed decisions about how to best position your business for success.

* * *

Customer Delivery Strategy - Often generically lumped in with Operations, Customer Delivery is the function of getting raw resources brought into the business, converted to value, and provided to the customer. This can be actual products, project-based work, or even services, such as consulting. A good customer delivery strategy is essential for ensuring that your customers are happy with your products or services. There are a few key components to a successful customer delivery strategy, including:

- Delivery Method: You need to decide how you will deliver your products or services to your customers. Will they be shipped directly to them, or will they have to come to you? Is it information served through a self-paced website, or a classroom setting?
- Product Creation: Will you create bespoke products or services upon order, or will you offer options generically packaged?
- Customer Communication: Do you offer support after the product or service is received? Will your customers have access to top-notch customer support, or will there be an extensive self-help forum? Also consider

who owns the client touches at each part of their customer journey.

If you want to ensure that your customers are happy with your products or services, you need a solid customer delivery strategy in place. By following the tips above, you can create a delivery strategy that will meet the needs of your customers and help keep them coming back for more.

* * *

Accounting Strategy - Accounting is the process of recording, classifying, and summarizing financial transactions to provide information that is useful in making business decisions. It can be used to assess the financial performance of a company, make predictions about the future, and measure the success of business strategies.

Developing a good accounting strategy that considers Generally Accepted Accounting Principles (GAAP) is essential to ensure the accuracy and consistency of financial reporting. Developing strategies that comply with GAAP requires careful consideration of all aspects of accounting, including revenue recognition, inventory valuation, accrued liabilities, fixed assets, cash flow statements and more. Record-keeping and internal controls should also be incorporated into the strategy to ensure accuracy and reliability of financial data. Moreover, a good accounting strategy should strive for transparency in both reporting to external stakeholders as well as within the organization itself. Organizations can foster an atmosphere of trust with their stakeholders and cultivate strong relationships with them by using clear language and understandable terminology.

Even if you are following GAAP, there are many ways to customize your accounting strategy to fit the specific needs of your business. For instance, you may choose to adopt an inventory costing method that best suits your operations or decide on the criteria for recognizing revenue. You could also consider different ways of performing periodic financial reviews and audits to ensure accuracy and compliance with both internal processes as well as external requirements. Additionally, by creating a system for monitoring and tracking financial performance, you can improve the effectiveness of your overall accounting strategy.

Having a well-defined accounting strategy in place will help organizations minimize errors, create value and ensure compliance with all applicable regulations. It is also important to be consistent in the implementation of the strategy, as changes in any element can affect all other aspects of accounting, from reporting to taxation. By taking these steps, organizations can ensure that their financial data is accurate and reliable and that they are well-positioned for future success.

* * *

Human Capital Strategy - When it comes to human resources strategy, there are a few key components to consider. One of the most important is hiring. You need to have a process in place for finding and recruiting the best talent for your company. You also need to have a system for onboarding new employees and getting them up to speed quickly.

Consider the previous strategies you've already developed. Each one of those may have a plan for hiring new employees. Take into account the timeliness of getting resources in place before hiring. Additionally, plan for employee turnover.

Benefits are another important part of human resources strategy. You need to offer benefits that are attractive to potential employees, and you need to keep up with changes in the benefits landscape. For example, flexible work schedules, health insurance, and paid time off are all benefits that should be considered when developing your human capital strategy.

Additionally, you need to have documented policies for your employees to follow. These might include policies on time off, performance management, and conflict resolution. Documented policies help guide employees and give them clear expectations for their work and behaviors. A good Human Capital strategy involves creating and reviewing HR policies.

A sound human capital strategy will take all these factors into account in order to create an effective and efficient workforce. By hiring the right people, providing competitive benefits, and creating clear policies, you can ensure that your human capital strategy is a success.

* * *

Leadership Strategy - In order to develop a successful leadership strategy, there are a few key elements that you should consider. One of the most important is developing a strong organizational culture. Culture refers to the values, beliefs, and behaviors that are shared by people in an organization. Strong organizational culture can help create alignment between employees and leaders, making your team more productive and efficient.

In order to create this alignment, you need to make sure that your leadership strategy includes a focus on communication and collaboration. You can do this by using tools such as employee surveys, surveys of customers and clients, retreats with leaders to brainstorm solutions, and more. By encouraging communication between employees and managers in your organization, you can ensure that organizational culture is strong, and your leadership strategy is a success.

Your leadership strategy should also consider leadership development. This can be particularly important if you have a fast-growing company and there are new positions popping up all the time. Leadership development involves creating a training program for managers and grooming potential leaders to take on more responsibility as their skills develop. Leaders who are well trained and developed will help strengthen your organizational culture, which is essential to success.

These are just a few of the key elements to consider when developing a leadership strategy for your company. By focusing on organizational culture, communication, and development, you can ensure that your leaders are as effective as possible and that your team is aligned behind your vision for success.

As you develop your departmental strategies, be sure to continuously refer to your company strategy and never let your department heads or managers dictate or force change to the company strategy. Your departmental strategies must support and align with the company strategy for them to be truly effective and useful. This means that they need to help you achieve the company's overall mission, vision, and goals.

Strategic financial plan

The importance of having a strong strategic financial plan for an entrepreneur cannot be overstated. By having a well-thought out and carefully organized financial plan in place, entrepreneurs can be better equipped to succeed in their business endeavors and maximize the return on their investment. A good strategic financial plan helps entrepreneurs identify their goals, set realistic targets, and manage their resources and investments in an efficient manner. Additionally, it helps protect them from unforeseen financial risks and provides guidance in making informed decisions about their business's future.

Establishing an accurate budget for your business operations is essential. You should factor in all expenses including project start-up costs, research & development, marketing & promotion, materials & labor, inventory management, taxes & fees, and debt repayments. This will help you to keep track of how much money you need to spend each month and where it's going so that you can make informed decisions about where you can save or invest your funds instead.

Develop a financial forecasting plan by creating detailed spreadsheets that project your expected revenues and expenses over the course of the next year or two. This will allow you to anticipate any potential problems that may arise with cash flow, as well as helping you to effectively manage your resources and investments to minimize risk and maximize returns.

Reviewing insurance policies is important for entrepreneurs to do regularly. As business conditions change, so does the need for different types of insurance coverage such as property damage, liability, product recall costs and more. Having adequate protection ensures that your business assets are secure in case of an unforeseen event.

Analyzing risks associated with each opportunity carefully is always wise before making any decisions. This involves researching the potential returns, as well as understanding any potential risks that may arise from the venture. It is important to understand what you could potentially lose should the investment not go according to plan.

Entrepreneurs can ensure they are better equipped to succeed in their business endeavors by making informed decisions supported by sound financial planning. Ultimately, this will help to increase cash flow and maximize returns on investments over time.

* * *

Your company's Vision should be written down and often communicated to your team; it's the foundation of where you want your business to go. The strategy is what creates and improves upon your value machine. The budget makes both of those things possible. Your strategy, vision, and budget play an integral role in what success looks like for your business.

A clear vision and actionable strategy are essential for any company looking to be successful. Without these two things in place, it becomes difficult to make decisions, prioritize tasks, and stay on track. By taking the time to develop a well-defined vision and strategy, you'll put your business in a much better position to succeed.

Lastly, if it seems that any of these strategy guides are a bit light – they are! Each one could be a book in itself! If you struggle in any of these areas, reach out to my organization using the links at the end of this book.

*"You have to remember to understand
the value of all your business branches.
In the end, you want a business where
everything is as strong as it can be."*

*— Pooja Agnihotri, 17 Reasons Why
Businesses Fail :Unscrew Yourself From
Business Failure*

Where You Need to be

A business leader has wishes and dreams. It's important to integrate your desires into your company, but it's also important to realize that a company is bigger than yourself. There are employees and stakeholders that are affected by the decisions made by you and the actions made by the company.

It's equally important to remember that our thoughts and desires can be flawed, swayed by outside forces, or affected by our emotions. Our knowledge is limited and, as a business owner, not knowing the questions to ask can cause severe consequences.

When considering the future of your company you must also consider that growth puts your company at more risk than it had when it was smaller. Many times, compliance standards have become a requirement. As your company grows, these standards become more difficult to meet. It is important to understand the law and regulations that govern your industry in order to maintain compliance.

Employment at your company changes with growth as well. As employees change from wearing many hats to limited responsibilities, it can be disorienting for both the employee and the rest of the company. Hiring more employees also brings in more requirements and formal practices. Timeliness is key when hiring a growing workforce.

As you plan, don't forget to consider what that growth means for you, your company, and your employees.

Second opinion

While it's great to come up with a long-term strategy for your company, it is equally important to make sure that these strategies are profitable and viable within your target market. You want to make sure that customers actually want to buy your products or services, but you also want to make sure that the tools, products, or materials that you may need in order to produce that value will be there.

Your investment in the future of your company is a bet on your determination and ability to execute. It is dependent on the employees, third party providers, and resources that your business counts on. It is at the mercy of the global and local economy. It truly is a gamble that will rely on many things. Let me tell you about three horse gamblers, Robert, Susan, and Thomas.

* * *

Robert is an amateur horse gambler. He has a few friends that made some good money by betting on horses and decided that he would do the same. Robert places his bet on a horse that shares the same name as his favorite pet dog, Speedy. You see, Speedy passed away a year ago today. It's a fairly unusual name for a dog. Being here on this day and seeing a horse named Speedy couldn't possibly just be coincidence. Robert tells his friends of his idea to put all his money on Speedy. He tells them about the similarities in the situation and they notice that very few people are betting on this horse. They all excitedly agree that the planets must be aligned. Robert feels great about his odds and places his bet. Unsurprisingly, Robert loses all his money on that horse.

Just like Robert, there are a surprisingly large number of business owners that invest their life savings into an idea based on the feeling that it couldn't possibly lose. They came up with a nice logo and a name for the business that is a tribute to a family member or a song they enjoyed on some special night. They get some positive encouragement from a few close friends and feel that their business idea is bulletproof. Pair that with the stories that we are constantly fed about how millionaires became rich and powerful by simply never giving up and you get a headstrong business owner that is likely to fail.

In the neighboring suite is Susan. Susan is a slightly more experienced horse gambler. Susan's company often hosts client events at the horse track. Not only has she gambled on horses before, but she's been alongside some of the people who have won big money. She learned to look at the other horses and compare their past performance. She chooses a horse based on its past winnings. She might even consider when that horse raced last and the jockey's performance on that particular horse. Susan hasn't quite figured out how others seem to be so sure, but she does pretty well for herself in the long run. Most of the time she loses but she wins enough to keep playing. This evening, she wins a modest amount of money.

Susan is like most business owners that are reading this book. While she can still be a little emotional about which horse she decides to finally place her bet on, she is at least staying away from making fully emotional decisions. Many business owners have learned that looking at financial reports, their customer retention, and their inventory turnover is important to success. A few may have even started their business with those processes in place. They are keeping a close eye on what is going on within their business.

Several years ago, Susan hired John, a young accountant out of college. She knew that monitoring her business was important and wanted to make sure she had the time to work in the other areas of her business. John's work allowed her to keep a close eye on the finances of her company.

Susan's company is successful in that they have managed to stay in business and keep their core employees. But sometimes business isn't as good. There have been a few times in the last five years where they have had to lay a few employees off and tighten their belt. It wasn't necessarily because of anything they did, she thinks. It just happens. With just a little more practice, though, maybe her business will be more successful. Right?

Thomas pulls his phone out of his tailored suit pocket and puts it up to his ear. He has been coming to the horse races for several years after being introduced to it by a joint venture partner. Just like Susan, he used to see a lot of ups and downs with his business. Tired of the downward trends, he began partnering with other companies and utilizing consultants to help him make informed decisions. He realized long ago that success couldn't come by himself.

After a few minutes, he puts the phone down and places his bet. More often than not, Thomas finds success. This evening did not disappoint him.

At the stables, Joe shoves his phone back into his coat pocket. Joe has been around horses for years. Growing up on an equestrian ranch, he learned how to train horses from the time they were two years old until they were sold to the owners who raced them. Joe has enough experience to be able to look at a horse and feel its muscles to know if it is fit for a race. He can tell by mannerisms if the horse is determined to win a race or if it is just not in the mood. Joe is one of the best horse race experts in the country and is well compensated by Thomas.

We've all read countless articles about the CEOs that took a small startup to a million-dollar company. Their vision was extraordinary, their strategy was genius. None of these successful businesspeople got there alone. Just outside of the limelight of those visionaries are the COOs, consultants, and other experts that were paid to help the millionaire tweak his idea into that million-dollar strategy.

Thomas, like Susan, also believes in keeping a close eye on the metrics within his company. He even shares a deep passion for his company just like Robert. What sets Thomas apart from Robert and Susan is that Thomas sought out external help for his company. Thomas realized that he isn't an expert in all aspects of business and brought on others who are more experienced and knowledgeable, not just in his industry, but those who recognize risks and opportunities in the market. Thomas proactively sought out executive advisors at the C-level to provide guidance and direction for his company, which relies heavily on external factors such as other industries, markets, and macroeconomic trends.

When Thomas talked to his CIO about his strategy, he learned that while the Customer Relationship Management (CRM) software he was currently using was great, another CRM was about to release integrations that could automate tasks between his CRM and his enterprise resource planning tool. Because Thomas migrated from his old CRM to the new, he was able to get grandfathered in with great pricing while increasing efficiency with automations.

Thomas learned from his CFO that another industry was destined for a downturn and would likely be laying off employees. Planning for growth, Thomas worked with his Human Resources Officer and COO to create training and processes that would translate activities that he needed done in a way that employees from that other industry could understand. Thomas was able to redirect employees that were flooding into the unemployment pool into his business with very little lost from the learning curve.

His Chief Revenue Officer was able to help Thomas devise a more effective sales strategy that allowed him to hire several employees that could help him increase his sales. He also focused on expanding the company's digital presence to reach more potential customers and target new markets. With this strategy, Thomas was able to significantly increase his business' revenue and expand his customer base.

Thomas heavily relied on his COO to prioritize and plan for all these activities so that his company could scale quickly without imploding. Rather than relying on himself, he was able to utilize the expertise from his C-suite to modify his company strategy to be successful.

Compliance

Not including compliance in your business strategy could be very costly. PCI, HIPPA, SOC, ISO or other compliance standards may be required once your company reaches a certain size or reaches into certain markets.

Implementing security measures, employee training, and process control as an afterthought is exponentially more difficult, time-consuming, and costly. While compliance may seem like needless red tape, most of the requirements are there to protect your customers and your company. What business owner wouldn't want that?

* * *

I was brought on as an operations consultant for a large company with international reach. Over a decade prior, this company was the forefront of an electronic payment system for millions of transactions per day. Now, they have clients using their technologies in several states and a few other countries. The company had been requested to prove their compliance for PCI (payment card industry) by the banks and credit card companies by participating in an audit and obtaining PCI certification.

By this time, obtaining PCI certification would not only cost thousands of dollars, but would completely derail customer acquisition projects and software development efforts for the next iteration of their system which was meant to beat their competition to the patent.

I participated in meetings with the client and banks to curtail PCI compliance. The company had been arguing that compliance shouldn't be their responsibility, it was the responsibility of their clients who were receiving the payments. They argued that the payment card processor was responsible for PCI. They even tried sweet talking the banks into letting it slide until the next iteration of their system was out.

The company was in a hard spot, but the banks wouldn't budge. Finally, the largest bank offered an ultimatum. Become PCI compliant by the end of the year or lose the ability to process credit cards.

It took a grueling 8 months to obtain PCI compliance. They passed on the first try – both of those nearly unheard of for a PCI audit of that size.

It had cost the company millions of dollars, long nights and weekends from the staff, and turnover in key leadership positions. The biggest cost was the opportunity to reach the patent before the competitors. They didn't make it. Their rival beat them to it.

Their original strategy was to be a high value option to their clients. They are now forced to be the low-cost competitor.

Any expert that works in compliance will tell you that compliance is always important. Most business owners think that when their company is too small it doesn't matter. Even if that were true, you must plan for compliance if you are planning for growth. Failure to prepare for regulatory compliance can cost your business dearly.

At the heart of every compliance regulation is a desire to protect customers and keep their data safe. As a business owner, you should value the same principles. Compliance can seem like an unnecessary burden, but it is there to protect your customers and your business.

Employees

Any business owner knows that employees can be one of the largest causes of stress in their business. Most business owners feel they never have enough employees or never have the right employees. A few considerations when planning for the future of your business are how you will hire additional employees, how you will train, when you will hire them, and how they will fit into your company machine.

When hiring new employees, consider the company culture and the needs of the business. Be specific in the job description and screen candidates properly. This includes reviewing their resume, checking references, and conducting interviews. Ask questions that will help you determine if the candidate has the skills and personality that would be a good fit for your company. Create a job description that is specific and accurately reflects the duties of the position. This will help to screen candidates and ensure that they are qualified for the position.

Provide new employees with proper orientation and training. This will help them learn the ropes and understand your company's culture. It will also help them develop the skills they need to be successful in their new position. Be thorough when it comes to training employees in documented business processes and procedures. The training should include an overview of the process, how and when to use it, and any relevant notes or exceptions. Practice the process. This will help employees learn how to complete it correctly and ensure that it is done in a timely manner.

Not considering when to hire employees is one of the most common mistakes a company makes. The company needs to be ready to hire, meaning that the processes and resources that an employee needs should be at least mostly available. Far too often do companies hire new employees without the support systems in place and expect the employee to just wing it. It sets them up for failure as well as the company. Plan your projects, plan for your new clients. Know when you're going to need employees and prepare for it in advance.

Employees aren't just cogs in a system. They are people that you are giving responsibilities to and tasks to carry out. Plan the organization of your employees. Create an accountability chart that describes each role in your business. This is different than an organization chart. An organization chart shows who reports to whom. An accountability chart is a diagram that describes the various company functions and the roles within. It's a nuanced difference, but the focus is on the role of the employee, not seniority. Because an accountability chart is role based, you may have employees occupying more than one spot. This helps you identify areas where you may need to make your next hires as the roles become more complex or time consuming.

Organizational Chart

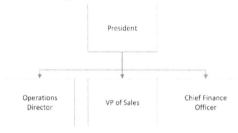

Accountability Chart

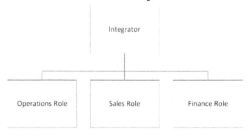

Frameworks Consulting, 2022

* * *

It is important for business owners to consider the future of their company and how that growth will affect all aspects of operations. Growth can bring with it more complex compliance standards, which must be met in order to protect customers and the business itself. Additionally, hiring employees correctly and effectively should also be a priority when planning for the future as this can help ensure smooth transitions into new roles and responsibilities. Finally, remember to keep customer needs top-of-mind while developing strategies so that your products or services are viable within your target market. You will set yourself up for success by taking these considerations into account before making any big decisions about growing your business!

"Believing there is a bridge from where you are to where you want to go is 99% of the battle. The other 1% is to cross it."

— *Richie Norton*

Bridging the Gap

You will have found gaps that lower the effectiveness of your company now and will decrease the chances of successfully reaching your goals as you progress through these exercises. This can be a source of pain and anxiety for a business owner. It may seem like an impossible task to close these gaps. As the saying goes, it's best to eat the elephant one bite at a time.

We're now at the stage of our system where we can categorize, organize, and prioritize the things that need to happen in your business to make it run more smoothly and begin to conquer your short-term goals. There are many different tools you can use to help with this process, including software programs and organizational systems, but a simple spreadsheet will get the job done.

Begin with a list of the gap items that you've found so far. Categorize the list by department. Is this a sales and marketing gap, financial management, or does it encompass the whole company? Knowing which department of your company will own this gap will help you assign managers to the issue and give them accountability to make sure it gets it done.

Now, you can organize the gap issues into groups. Determine if there are any gap issues that can be combined and solved together, or if there may be an issue that should really be broken into 2 or 3 issues. Be descriptive of what the root of the problem really is and what the issue will solve.

Finally, you can prioritize the issues based on the risk level to the business. We can calculate this based on the impact of the issue and the probability that the issue will affect the productivity of the business. You can assign a number or rating to each issue and then graph them to see at a glance which issues should be addressed immediately. It is important to think logically through this step and not let emotions or personal feelings get in the way. Be honest with yourself. For instance, you may have identified your CRM to be a big problem. Perhaps it is keeping you from achieving your sales goals and bringing in revenue. However, you also know that you've spent many hours and a lot of money on it so far. It may be tempting to put it at the bottom of your list or say that it's not a problem. You would be doing yourself and your business a disfavor by not addressing the issue properly.

Once you've categorized, organized, and prioritized your business gap issues, you can begin to take steps to close those gaps and reach your short-term business goals. Start with the issues that are identified as high risk. These are the issues that your business needs to address right away in order to continue moving forward and keep your profits rolling. Each issue will give people in your company an action item to work on the business or may be a full project. Some may even need outside help. Look at each issue and discuss with your team the various solutions that could solve these issues. Choose the issues that make the most sense for your company at this point in its lifecycle.

Creating your options

You will likely come up with multiple solutions to each of the gap issues when working with your team to solve the issues. Be creative but spend some time researching potential solutions. You don't want to make poor decisions for your company because you came up with one solution and stopped there or implemented a solution that just creates more problems.

Consider reaching out to outside resources, such as other business owners you may network with or professional consultants who can offer their knowledge and expertise on the subject. Doing your research will give you a better idea of what options are out there and how to approach the problem.

Once you have a few solid ideas, take some time to create a plan of action and know to whom you would assign various responsibilities. You will need to compare options based on the full picture when choosing the best path. Budget, time, and focus will be critical factors to consider. Some options may seem like an extremely quick fix but can create long-term problems that are more expensive over time. Consider resources that you have in the business as well as vendors that could implement solutions for you.

Project budget

It's important to think about all the associated costs when it comes to budgeting a project. This includes the cost of materials, labor, and overhead. You'll also need to factor in any administrative or support costs. It's important to be realistic about how much the project will cost and how long it will take to complete.

Budgeting for a project can seem like a daunting task, but it becomes a little more manageable if you break it down into smaller steps. The first step is to determine the scope of the project. What needs to be done and what are the desired outcomes? Once you have a better understanding of what needs to be done, you can start estimating the cost of each component of the project.

You'll also need to decide how you will finance the project. Do you have enough cash on hand or will you need to borrow money? If you're borrowing money, what are the interest rates and terms? How does that impact your budget?

Above all, it is essential to stay within budget. Remember the critical elements you took into account when constructing your business's strategic financial plan? Don't ignore them and make sure not to exceed what you have allocated for spending. You were taking everything into account as a whole picture when you made that budget. Oftentimes, this is where managers might try to justify the need for a bigger budget. They might say that the company has been bringing in more revenue or try to re-argue the importance of the project. Changes to the budget can be made, but you need to take it back to the top and think strategically again.

Plan your work and work your plan.

You can create a preliminary budget for the project once you have all this information gathered. Remember that this is just an estimate and may change as you move forward with planning. You'll want to go over the budget throughout the project to make sure you're still on track.

Choosing the best path

To choose the best path to close your gaps, set some criteria for the options you will consider. For instance, how much revenue would the option bring in and what are the risks to your business? What is the cost of the option and if it succeeds? What is the potential profit? Will this option make you money or save you money? You will likely have to do some research to get the information you need, but this will help you decide which option is best for your company.

Next, choose the option that best meets your business needs and has the potential to be the most successful. Consider all the possible options, but make sure you are thinking about what will give you the best return on your investment. As previously mentioned, it's important to consider the focus of your team as well. While it may be tempting to have your team self-implement a system, they may not be the best option. Your team still has a job to do. They may be experts at using the system, but they may not be the best at implementing it.

Once you have decided on a course of action, it's time to implement your solution. Work with your team to put a plan into action and get it off the ground. This can be a long process, so you will need to set clear goals and timelines, tracking your progress as you go. Make sure you keep everyone involved in the issue up-to-date and on the same page so that everyone is working towards the same goals.

Make sure that you stay on top of things as you implement your solutions and work to close the business gap. Update your customers and team regularly about the progress, and don't be afraid to make changes if needed. With some time and effort, you can reduce the gap in your business and start reaching your short-term goals.

* * *

By following the steps outlined in this chapter, you can identify your company's gaps and develop a plan to close them. You should think through each gap issue carefully and be honest about its risk level and potential solutions. Once you have identified the issues that need to be addressed, prioritize them based on their impact on business productivity. Then start working with your team to come up with creative solutions that will reduce costs while increasing revenue or saving money for the company. Finally, set some criteria for any options you are considering so that you make an informed decision when it comes time to budgeting projects. Closing gaps in your business becomes much easier with these tips in mind!

George Mayfield

"In business partnerships, it's important to do your due diligence and eliminate as much risk from the deal as possible."

— Hendrith Vanlon Smith Jr, CEO of Mayflower-Plymouth

You Can't Afford Trial and Error

You really can't afford to just try a vendor and see if they work out unless you are a company with vast resources and nothing left to invest your profits in. If that is you, please, let's have a talk and figure out how you pulled that off!

Let's say you bring in a bookkeeper and you find out three months later that your books haven't been kept up to date in the way that you need. Now you're trying to supply documents for a business loan and must go back and redo all your accounting records. The time and effort to go back and fix your books is going to cost thousands of dollars. Not to mention that now you have to spend time finding another bookkeeper. You should have been using a great vendor that matched your business perfectly from the start.

Hiring a vendor should be much like hiring an employee. The hiring process for many companies requires multiple rounds of interviews and tests. They might include personality assessments, background checks, and even drug screenings. All these hoops that a job applicant must go through to simply be considered are quite overwhelming, and oftentimes, unnecessary.

On the other hand, that same company may only meet with an outside company once before they are hired for a project or service. What is the reasoning behind this? Whether you hire someone or bring in an external firm - they both provide services that benefit your organization. Shouldn't you look at the vetting process of a provider in much the same way?

***

Calvin found an opportunity to start his transportation business. Investing in a few trucks, he was contracted to handle last mile deliveries for a large logistics company. He was great at managing his company and had very little delivery mishaps. His business continued to grow, gaining more contracts. Calvin hated accounting, though. He always struggled through the paperwork.

Finally, he decided to ask some of the people in his network about someone he could hand the accounting tasks off to. He heard about a local bookkeeping company that other small businesses in his area raved about. They claimed that this company always kept their books up to date and always turned their reports in on time.

Calvin decided to try out this bookkeeping company and see if they could work for his growing business. He gladly handed over control of his books and left everything up to the bookkeeping company. Payroll seemed to happen on time and accurately. Vendors never complained about late payments. Calvin felt that turning over the accounting functions of his company was the best thing he ever did.

Then something unexpected happened - Calvin got a letter from the IRS about a discrepancy. Calvin asked the bookkeeping company about it and was told that they would take care of it. He was relieved to hear that! However, a few months later, he received another letter. Calvin realized that he would have to investigate it himself. After a long and stressful week, he came to understand that the bookkeeping company was doing little more than paying checks using their payment system. When it came to the books, it was a mess!

Calvin had to spend a lot of time fixing the mistakes that this bookkeeping company made, and he lost valuable time that could have been spent growing his business.

In the end, Calvin decided to find a new bookkeeping company that would be able to match the specific needs of his business. He searched for a bookkeeper who could keep up with the fast-paced nature of his company, who could keep his books updated and accurate, and who would be able to provide helpful reports that he could use to make better business decisions. This time, he asked for references from people currently using their services. He checked his state's board of public accountancy and made sure that they were properly licensed and didn't have any complaints on file. The process took a bit longer to onboard the bookkeeping company, but it was worth it.

Looking back, Calvin realized that he had made a costly mistake by not doing the necessary research to find a bookkeeper who would be a good fit for his business. He learned that a good vetting process is absolutely necessary for third party providers. If you spend so much time and effort to make sure an employee can do the work they were hired to do, shouldn't the same be said of other businesses that are doing a service for you?

Vetting service providers

The process of vetting a service provider is essential if you want to find the right fit for your business. Some of the key points are to make sure they can do the work you need done and that the company can blend with your company, almost seeming like an extension or department.

Make sure the service provider is qualified to do the work. Check to see if the service provider is licensed, if needed. You should also look to see if the provider is certified or specialized in some way, as that can be a good sign of quality.

Obtain referrals from other businesses or people who have used the service provider before. This can give you a better idea of how the service provider works and if they are able to meet the specific needs of your business. Once you get those referrals, be sure to have some questions ready and make the calls.

Find out how long the service provider has been in business and check their track record. You don't want to work with a new or inexperienced company, as that could end up being more of a headache than it's worth.

Request proof of insurance and investigate what type of coverage they have. This can be especially important if you're dealing with something sensitive or critical to your company. It's not uncommon to have a copy of their policy and to talk through the details with them.

Ask about the service provider's policies and procedures, especially regarding safety and security measures. Whether this should cover your company's data or safety around your personnel, it is important to know what the service provider's policies are in case something happens.

Find out what kind of customer support or assistance the service provider offers after hours or in case of an emergency situation. This is especially important if you need quick support and assistance, or if their support will reflect onto you with your customers.

Get a written contract or agreement from the service provider that outlines all terms, conditions, and pricing information before you agree to use their services. Ensure that the provider has the bandwidth to take on your company's work.

Ask about the provider's mission and culture. Do they share the same values as your company? Are their general working styles and procedures similar to what you are used to? Not only do you want to avoid companies with an overly dissimilar culture, partnering with a company that is a better match can help ensure efficiency in working together.

Lastly, do a bit of background checking to see if the company is experiencing any issues. Make sure there aren't any public cases against the company or cases the company is raising against someone else. Check with the secretary of state to make sure their tax status is current and that there aren't any revocations. Other searches you may find valuable are Dunn & Bradstreet, Whois, Google Business, and Yelp. Look at these results as part of the whole picture and keep an open dialog with the company. Their response to any questions you raise may tell you more about the company than anything you've found.

Get what you pay for (and pay for what you get)

Cory was the owner of an employee staffing company. From the start, he was a difficult client. I was pretty new in my consulting career and put up with a lot more than I should have. Cory had an array of passionate emotions that could manifest in volatile ways. You never knew what kind of mood you'd be walking into as soon as you stepped foot in his office. He demanded that his office be kept in pristine condition and expected complete obedience from everyone who worked around him. He relished being a leader that commanded and controlled for many years, unaware of the possibility of evolving his approach and how that could serve him.

Adorning the main cubicle room was a custom-made banner that outlined exactly what his employees should strive for; ten essential expectations to be achieved. "Always be early to work", and "Be prepared to stay late" were among them. One of the lines that stuck out to me most was, "do more than what you are paid to do". That banner really set the tone for how he operated. His employees were paid below the industry standard and, unsurprisingly, had a high turnover. He had a policy to never pay full price for anything, yet he expected high quality service.

Somehow Cory had recently gotten a contract with a large corporation, and I was brought in to manage the project and help him expand his office. He was already on his third contractor that was brought in to break down the wall between the current office and the empty office next door. He vented his frustration, claiming that contractors were untrustworthy and had tried to deceive him out of more money. They were either constantly cutting corners or trying to charge him more money than they originally agreed on. At the time, the team and I believed him. We assured him that we would help him with an expansion plan and manage vendors that would do great work for him to the quality that he wanted.

The location and architecture of the building made running cable problematic. The internet cables that were provided to the building would only support low bandwidth. The internet service provider had given him a quote to run fiber to the building, but the owner thought that the price was too high. He was having somebody in his family dig a trench to the building so that fiber cable could be laid. At least that was the idea. No ground had been broken yet, and the cousin was either stuck at getting permits or just being lazy, depending on the day anyone asked Cory about the status.

Our job was to help the business with the expansion plans within the walls of the building. Rather than daisy chaining internet connections from each office tenant to the far end of the building where he was, we advised running a high bandwidth internet cable to the demarcation point (where internet came to the building) directly. This would limit possible failures as well as provide better security and higher quality. Cory, of course, agreed. He wanted blazingly fast internet and didn't want any further problems.

I tend to have several companies that I can refer to depending on the level of quality a customer wants and their budget. Regardless of the level of their price, or the way they package their services, they would always be carefully vetted. This ensures that they possess the necessary insurance, a proven track record and other credentials to guarantee their legitimacy. I always advise my client to investigate those vendors and let them make the best choices on their own. To ensure they choose correctly, I recommend that each vendor explain their services in detail so that the client can understand exactly what is being offered before making a final decision. Three different low-voltage cabling companies were given the opportunity to provide Cory with a quote.

The IT company that was brought in was already having a difficult time with the client. They were tasked with updating the computers so that they could work with the company server and the software that his company used. None of the computers were the same model or even brand.

Most of them, the owner bragged, were bought for a steal on craigslist. The IT provider tried to talk him into purchasing new, yet modest, workstations for his employees to use. The software required a secure connection to the server which meant that the computers needed to be on the newest version of Windows Pro. Most of the computers were using older Windows Home versions.

The owner was aware of the software's requirements. However, he had no desire to throw away all the money he spent on the Craigslist computers and replace them with brand-new computers. The IT company was spending hundreds of man hours per week with multiple people working on these computers to try to get them to work with the newer versions of Windows. Many of the computers didn't have the correct amount of RAM.

"Just make it work", Cory would tell them. The IT company ended up having to cannibalize RAM from old computers, or even rebuild old computers themselves just to make it work. It was obvious that the IT company was losing money on the deal, but they thought if they could just get this done, the client would be happy, and they'd have a client for life.

The rest of the project was just more of the same; trying to do a lot with a little. Cubicles, furniture, door keycard access -- he wanted the best of the best on some things but would be cheap on others and there was no rhyme or reason for it. Working with this client was far from a positive experience, and their meetings were something I dreaded on a regular basis. Then, one day, it came to a head. It was sometime in the evening, and I was in a grocery store with my family. Cory called and I knew if I didn't pick up, I would get an angry email. So, I answered the phone.

It was difficult to understand what I was hearing at first. The man was yelling so loud into his phone that my family could hear. I even saw a couple of strangers look over at me. I had to hold the phone at arm's length. Cory was upset because the cabling vendors I had sent to him had all withdrawn their quotes. All three of them. They were all trying to rob him, and I must be in on it. I calmly listened to what I was hearing and told Cory that I would call them and fix the problem. After a bit more yelling and choice language, he abruptly hung up the phone. I called each of the vendors and got similar stories. Two of them had already done some small job, "to prove themselves" and hadn't been paid. All three of them were similarly yelled at when they submitted their quote. That was the day that I learned how to fire a client.

The next day, I sent a kindly worded email to Cory explaining that our business was incompatible and that we would not be continuing our relationship. To express my sincerest apologies for placing them in an uncomfortable situation, I separately invited the three vendors out to lunch on me. I never wanted to be thought of as someone who would refer a company to a client like that. I vowed to never work for a client like that ever again.

The IT company stuck it out for a few more months before they left as well. I think it was about nine or ten months later that I heard that Cory's company was no longer in business. I'm not sure why and I didn't really care. It was bound to happen though.

***

There are two sides to compensation. You want to make sure that you're getting the right value for the money that you are paying for, but you also want to make sure that you are paying them fairly. Make sure that there are clear expectations for the work you need completed, the timeliness, and how it should be done. Keep in mind that working with a vendor is an investment for both you and for them.

Just as you develop Key Performance Indicators for your company, it is important to put KPIs in place for your vendors. You will find it useful to make data-driven decisions with your vendors and make sure that they continue to perform for you. Those KPIs will help identify areas where improvement is needed and indicate if objectives are being achieved. KPIs also enable companies to measure vendor effectiveness across different projects or workflows, keeping vendors accountable for their performance.

You will also want to make sure that your contract includes the key deliverables that you expect from the vendor. These deliverables should be clearly defined and meet your company's needs. Any additional goals or objectives that you may have will need to be negotiated with the vendor and should be put into your contract.

To ensure that you are getting the best value for your dollar, do a bit of research on other vendors in the same space. This will give you a clear idea of what types of services they offer, and what the market rates are for those services. You'll be able to compare price quotes and find the best value for your company's needs.

Many businesses work a bit too hard to make sure they are getting as much value from their vendors as possible. Some managers will question every line on an invoice and make it their policy to question the price regularly. They see it as an accomplishment to beat them down on price but never stop to think if it's fair or how it will affect their company.

A good working relationship with your vendors is very important. The money you pay your vendor helps them grow and invest in their business. Think of your vendors as an extension of your company. If you stifled one of your department's budgets, you'd end up with poor work and bad morale. Your department would be weak and not effective at its functions or helping your company grow.

Similarly, if you continually beat your vendors down on price, you may end up with one of two bad situations. The vendor cuts corners, lowering the quality of their work as much as they can get away with without you noticing, or the vendor fires you. Losing a good vendor puts you back at square one and can cost you a lot of time and resources as you search for another vendor.

At the end of the day, your relationship with your vendors should be a partnership. Negotiate fairly, focus on the deliverables, and let them do what they are good at without micromanaging. With a strong working relationship, you'll get the best value for your company and help your vendors grow their business too.

Vetting a business service provider is an essential step in the process of bringing on a new vendor. Whether you're looking for a bookkeeping company, marketing agency, or payroll service, you need to make sure that they are the right fit for your business. By taking the time to vet a potential service provider, you can be confident that they will deliver the results you need and save you a lot of time and frustration in the long run.

* * *

Dave and Evie were a husband-and-wife team that grew tired of working in the grind in their prospective careers. Dave worked in the financial industry and Evie was a sales director for an insurance company. Through a mutual contact, they found out about a business that was going up for sale. It was a small medical software company that offered a very niche service in the medical field. They both thought that this would be a great opportunity to own their own business and take control of their life. Their children were now having grandchildren and they wanted to be able to travel to see them whenever they wanted and be able to spend time with their family.

They began running into problems shortly after buying this medical software company. The most visible problem was the building that came with the business. The previous owner had been operating a hobby business out of the building as well and had just let that go into disarray. The previous owner was a big fan of exotic fish. An expensive hobby to have, he decided to dabble in raising and selling exotic fish himself. The building that Dave and Evie inherited had several rooms with large saltwater tanks, many of them still full of water. The smell was horrendous. What's worse is that the servers that the software operated on were housed at that location. The couple didn't really have a lot of IT experience, but they knew that this was probably a bad idea.

They set out to clean up the building and get rid of the tanks. Carpet had to be replaced from where the tanks leaked, and it was a large expense to move the tanks off the property. Many of the walls had to be repainted and it took an effort to make the office smell somewhat normal.

They made the office as comfortable as possible with family pictures in their office and framed inspirational quotes on the walls. Their new business was really starting to feel like a home. However, that's when the next problem surfaced.

It turned out that there were several clients that were paying a monthly maintenance fee that had been made promises that never came to fruition. There were some major bugs in the software and some clients had requirements that had to be met that would require new features to be written into the code. Several of these clients, including the largest ones, were giving them notice that they were going to cancel their account.

Dave and Evie had no idea about these promises or any of the issues that the customers were facing. In all honesty, they thought they were buying a business that would run itself. "The software is already there, all you have to do is collect money every month", the old owner had told them. They reached out to the developer who was still working with the company on a contract basis. They began asking him about bug fixes and updates to the software. They were under the impression that he had a contractual obligation to support the software that he had written.

Dave and Evie soon found out that the previous owner had never paid him the agreed amount for the last version, and it was a large sum of money. Dave and Evie pleaded with him. They tried to get him to make the fixes so that the business wouldn't go under. They promised to pay him based on residuals. The developer wasn't going to budge. He wanted to get paid, as of course he should have. Asking nicely didn't work, so the couple tried being more aggressive. They pulled out verbiage from the contracts they found and tried to use that to incite him to comply.

However, he had a trick up his sleeve. He was the only one with the administrative password to any of the servers. He began threatening the couple saying that he would delete the code if he didn't get paid. Now the couple had a legal expense they didn't plan on, and they were getting desperate.

They had just taken loans against their home and retirement accounts just to purchase this business. They didn't have anything left to pay the developer, nor did they have any money to invest in the next version. The couple began looking for other developers, but they soon found that recreating this software from scratch would cost $300,000 to $500,000 and it would likely take over a year before it could even be used. There's no way their customers would wait that long.

Eventually, the couple happened to meet a young developer that had a similar product in a completely different industry. This developer had a small business of his own and was very talented and giving. At first glance, the issue that the couple was confronting seemed like a simple fix and an exciting challenge. He could retrofit some of the code that he already had to do what they needed to do for their customers, and it would be a new source of income for him.

Their prayers have been answered! Desperately they began work with the new developer to recreate their software based on his code. They signed an agreement to pay a significant amount of money for each of their client's users and the developer got to work. Evie was able to use her account management skills to quell most of their customers. She promised them that they would have a solution in just a few months and that it would be even better than their previous solution.

Dave and Evie found themselves facing a lot of problems because of a few root causes. For starters, they really had no idea what they were getting themselves into. As mentioned, neither one of them had ever worked in the software business and didn't really know what sort of things might need to be done on a regular basis to support a software as a service company. They weren't set up to answer technical support questions. They didn't get any software documentation from the owner prior to the sale. They didn't even know to ask about the servers that the software was housed on.

They bought a company without utilizing any expertise or consulting to make sure that they were getting a fair deal. They didn't perform the appropriate amount of due diligence before buying the company and they barely even learned that lesson.

They were already a month and a half into the new development project when they were asked by an outside consultant if they had done any due diligence on the developer. In a sudden panic, they called the developers office and set up a meeting where they would bring along their consultant to ask a few questions.

The developer, who had been a client of mine for a year and a half at that point, already had things in place to make sure they were compliant, and the projects were run in a structured project management office with quality assurance, testing parameters, and change control approvals prior to releasing any code. The consultant that they brought in was satisfied with the answers they got from the developer's company.

Dave and Evie were lucky, but it could have gone another way very easily, and it would have been too late. Their old system had already been migrated to the new developer's servers and the old servers were long gone. If things had gone any other way, they may have found themselves in the same, expensive mess!

* * *

Performing due diligence isn't a hard thing to do. It requires some forethought and maybe even a little awkwardness when you have to ask some uncomfortable questions. It's kind of like a doctor. You don't want to go in, but you know that it will be good for you and the health of your organization. In this case, the couple was just trying to do what was best for their company, and they were going about it the wrong way by not talking to any experts or doing any research of their own. If they would have reached out to a few industry experts, it may have saved them quite a lot of time and money.

George Mayfield

Making Progress

When it comes to working on your business and making progress to close gaps and allow your company to operate efficiently and effectively, you'll need to implement some organizational processes and structure that you may not have had before. Project Management standards are a good place to start. While a full-blown Project Management Office may be overkill for your business, there are some key guidelines that can help you manage your progress. Change management is also something that you should study so that you can make sure that your employees are comfortable with the changes you're implementing.

Working on your business (while still working in your business) can be a challenge, but if you take the time to plan things out carefully, you'll have much more success in the long run. You'll be well on your way to a successful outcome and a better overall experience for everyone with these tips for managing projects and managing change!

Project management overview

In the previous chapters, you read about organizing your business improvements into projects. Managing your projects is just as important as managing your company's core operations. You'll need someone in your company who is at least mostly focused on the project and a decent platform to track progress and issues.

Project management guidelines are essential for businesses who wish to effectively manage their projects. By following these guidelines, businesses can properly organize and execute their projects in a way that is efficient, cost-effective and yields successful results.

The first step in managing a project with Project Management guidelines is the creation of a project plan. A project plan should outline the goals of a project, as well as the steps that need to be taken to achieve those goals. This can involve creating timelines and milestones for each step of the process, outlining important tasks, and assigning resources to complete those tasks. It is essential to have a thorough understanding of the goals and objectives that need to be accomplished before starting any project.

Don't get discouraged by setbacks. When working on any project, it's important not to get discouraged if you encounter setbacks along the way. Instead, view these challenges as opportunities to learn and grow. It is important to include contingency plans in the project plan in case there are any issues or unexpected delays along the way.

Another key component of project management is collaboration. It is important to keep all stakeholders informed about the progress of a project so that they can provide feedback and help as needed.

Overall, following project management guidelines can help businesses successfully manage their projects and achieve their goals. By being organized, communicating efficiently, and utilizing the right tools and strategies, businesses can effectively lead their projects to success.

Change management

Change management is an essential component of success in any business. It is not only a process of managing change, but also a mindset that encourages embracing change and adapting to it. Innovation is becoming increasingly important for organizations and changing with the times has become a necessity. Companies that can adapt quickly and effectively will thrive in today's competitive environment.

There are several strategies you can use to ensure effective change management within your organization. The first step is to create a culture that is open to change, one that values flexibility and innovation. This means encouraging new ideas from employees of all levels and giving them resources they need to implement those ideas successfully. Be honest, transparent, and authentic with your employees in order to build trust with others and form meaningful relationships; it's important to have honest and open communication throughout the change process.

You should also create a solid plan for managing change. Develop processes for managing changes efficiently such as through regular meetings or check-ins where any concerns can be raised and addressed quickly. Give your employees a venue to openly and safely discuss how they feel about changes. Make sure to celebrate and recognize the successes of your employees throughout the change process in order to motivate them.

Understand that change happens slowly - and that's what you want! Change tends to be more successful when it's introduced gradually and with the support of your employees. Trying to force change quickly will lead to many problems such as resistance, confusion, and frustration. Instead, be patient with your employees and give them the time and space they need to adjust to change in their own way. Taking on change within your company in a purposefully calculated way gives you the opportunity to be aware of how the change is affecting all aspects of your company.

Finally, you should always strive to remain flexible, yourself, by remaining open-minded and fully aware of how the changes are impacting your company.

It is crucial that you adopt a change management mindset and implement strategies that support this approach in order to successfully navigate the ever-changing business landscape. By doing so, you will set your organization up for continued success in today's fast-paced world.

Tools and resources

One of the most important aspects of implementing project management standards and change management into your business is communication. You need to make sure that your employees are kept up to date on changes and have clear expectations of what's expected of them. Make sure you have a platform that everyone can use to track progress and stay on top of important updates. Additionally, make sure that your employees have the time and skillset to work on these projects aside from their other duties.

A good management platform will help you and your team stay on top of issues and tasks. It's generally not recommended to simply rely on email and absolutely not recommended to manage through "fly-bys" that distract your employees and is hard to track and ensure that employees understand the task and expectations. Implementing a digital project management tool or issue tracker will save you a lot of headaches down the road, as you're able to quickly spot any potential issues and address them before they become a problem.

Make sure you have enough resources in place to get the project completed on time.

Assigning an ever-increasing pile of tasks to your employees is a sure way to fail in implementing improvements to your company. Be aware of the time requirements of your project's tasks, especially if those employees are still performing other operational tasks. Even switching from operational tasks to project tasks can take some time for an employee to adjust and wrap their heads around the new task at hand. The ability to multitask is a lie we've all told ourselves. The human brain can only focus on one task at a time. Juggling too many different priorities can easily lead to mistakes or missed deadlines.

Whether it's people, money, or equipment – if you don't have the necessary tools to complete the project, it can negatively impact the outcome and cause problems for everyone involved.

Measuring progress

Project milestones are important checkpoints that allow you to measure your project's progress and ensure that it is on track. By definition, a milestone is "an event marking an important stage in the development of something." In the context of project management, milestones usually refer to major accomplishments or deliverables that need to be completed in order for the project to be considered a success.

There are many ways to measure against project milestones, but some common methods include measuring against budget, schedule, and scope. Additionally, you can use qualitative measures such as customer satisfaction or employee engagement surveys to gauge how well the project is going. It's important to have a variety of measures in place so that you can get a complete picture of how the project is progressing.

If you find that your project is falling behind schedule or over budget, then it's time to take corrective action. This could involve adjusting the schedule or budget, renegotiating with suppliers, or changing the scope of the project. You can avoid costly delays or even cancellation of the project altogether by taking corrective action early.

Monitoring established key performance indicators (KPIs) is an important part of any change management process. KPIs are a way to measure the success or effectiveness of changes that have been implemented and serve as indicators of how well your business is doing. Properly monitoring KPIs can help you identify areas for improvement and make sure that changes are affecting the company in a positive way.

While we've talked about having KPIs in various departments in your company, higher level KPIs are the most appropriate to see how changes are affecting your company as you implement various projects. Keep in mind that metrics like revenue or employee satisfaction may not trend in the direction you expect the same month the change was implemented. However, when these numbers are tracked over a longer period, they can provide valuable insight into how your company has benefited from the change.

Implementing changes in a business can be difficult, but by using tools like project management software and issue trackers, you can make the process easier. Measuring progress is important in order to ensure that the project stays on track, and

George Mayfield

setting milestones allows you to measure against budget, schedule and scope. Additionally, establishing key performance indicators early on helps you monitor the success of changes made to the company.

* * *

The golf cart industry is a lot more interesting than I would have originally thought. Most Americans prefer a nice, customized golf cart that they could show off to their friends or potential clients on the golf course. Yet, fleet golf carts need to be easy to maintain and cost effective, while still being able to endure the treatment that some of the patrons would put them through.

I was working with a client several years ago to help him through his expansion strategies. Andre was very business savvy and realized that in this industry, most of the business owners seemed to be older. Their technologies and processes were still operating as they did back in the 1970s. Together, we came up with a plan for development and growth.

We took a hard look at how his business operated and what could make it better. We built out the plan to improve his home location and put several key performance indicators in place that he monitored in an online dashboard. We built out documentation for processes and policies that made his business unique and successful. This manual could be utilized at each location with a section for site-specific policies and one-off procedures.

Gradually, Andre would pursue a golf cart sales and maintenance shop. Once the shop was acquired, he would slowly and methodically begin converting the shop to operate like his home store. Some employees would welcome the changes while others did not. The application of KPIs, accountability, and mandated processes didn't allow much room for employees to take advantage of the business. That was a big reason why some of these businesses were failing before and had been bought for such a low price.

The employees who welcomed the change were usually junior people who had ideas on how to improve the business, but no one had been listening to them before. Andre began giving these employees the tools they needed to help him turn continuously improve the business. And they now had KPIs keeping them accountable and focused on the improvements being made.

Not only was the home store's system distributed to other locations, but so were its strategies and plans for improving company operations. The system we implemented even allowed for the best of the employees' ideas to be implemented at the home store and trickle out to all the others.

Each location manager was responsible for sales and maintenance teams as well as administrative functions. Each of these teams had their own KPIs and each store had overarching KPIs. The owner was able to look at the performance of each location and compare week by week, month by month, quarter by quarter, and annually. He could tell which locations were most resistant to change and which stores and departments he needed to focus more management and resources on.

This setup also allowed him to understand market conditions for each location. Andre made the difficult decision to shut some locations down even after he had spent so much investment in them. The poorly trending KPIs and the lack of improvement despite time, effort, and money made him realize that the problem was the geographic market. Data showed that the business just couldn't operate in that location - at least not in the way he wanted it to. He did consider that the market at some locations perhaps might pick up, but having the data allowed him to make the best decisions.

* * *

Many times, a business owner looks at the investment they put into an idea and, along with ego, lets that make the decisions for them. This is a common cause of the escalation of commitment fallacy. The escalation of commitment fallacy is a cognitive bias where an individual continues to invest in a failing project despite the obvious risks and diminishing returns. It occurs when people are emotionally invested in something and overestimate their chances of success, even when all evidence suggests otherwise. This phenomenon is often seen in business ventures and projects where decisions are made based on past experiences, emotions, and individual preferences rather than objective data and rational analysis.

Andre was able to make his business idea a working strategy by taking an honest look at where his business was and where he knew it needed to go. He documented his processes and business plans and was able to monitor the progress because of the consistent measurements he took in his business. Using that as his formalized business plan, he was able to scale his business to many more locations. Through implementing these frameworks, Andre has grown his business exponentially and turned it into one of the most profitable operations around.

George Mayfield

"People might be skeptical about their ability to change if they're by themselves, but a group will convince them to suspend disbelief. A community creates belief."

— Charles Duhigg, The Power Of Habit: Why We Do What We Do In Life And Business

The Power of a Mastermind

A smart business owner knows that there is great value in pairing up with a mentor. A mentor can be someone that you can talk to about your business, anything going on within the business, or just life as a business owner. An experienced mentor can help you make decisions and choose the right course of action. A mentor can also be a confidant to help you feel less lonely as a business owner and help you have the confidence to do what needs to be done. Mentors are a great thing to have, but there are some weaknesses.

A mentor is typically just one person. They can only have the knowledge and experience from their own lifetime. Finding a mentor that worked within your industry seems like a good idea, and they may be very knowledgeable about problematic aspects that you may be dealing with. On the other hand, having a mentor that works in your industry can limit your creative thinking and problem solving in new ways.

They also have limited availability. It can be difficult to get a consistent meeting with your mentor. Oftentimes, due to the personal nature, the business owner may feel that they don't want to bother their mentor and their service goes unused. Eventually, the relationship will fizzle out.

A Mastermind is like having a group of people as your mentors. A mastermind group, coined way back in 1937 by Napoleon Hill in his book "Think and Grow Rich", takes advantage of the diverse experiences and knowledge of a group of people. It finds value in not just the wisdom of yourself, but from other members of the group freely discussing ideas and concepts.

"More gold has been mined from the brains of men than has ever been taken from the Earth."

– Napoleon Hill, Think and Grow Rich

Joining a mastermind gives you access to mentors in your industry, complementary industries, and dissonant industries. It gives you a diverse group of people with all kinds of expertise, experiences, and perspectives. You may be able to reach out at any given time for any kind of a problem you may have depending on how your Mastermind is set up.

There are many masterminds out there with all manner of focuses and strengths. One great mastermind to look into is 'Rock Your Life' with Craig Duswalt. His program focuses on having a rockstar mindset, both in your personal life and in business. Personally, I've experienced benefits that have helped in both, but I have also been close with several entrepreneurs in his program that have seen a tremendous improvement in their mindset which has allowed them to take advantage of opportunities that they previously lost motivation for. Getting this very book completed and published was largely due to my relationship with Craig.

bit.ly/FWRYL

Not without weaknesses of its own, a mastermind only gives you what you put into it. A mentor, for a time, may "babysit" you to make sure that you are staying on track. In a mastermind group, it's up to you to get and remain involved. A mastermind small group could help keep you accountable. We'll talk more about those later.

Competition

Watch out for those sneaky competitors that try to get into your Mastermind group. They will find out everything that you are doing wrong and take advantage of your weaknesses. They will steal your best ideas. They will take all your customers and leave you with nothing. Well, that's what most business owners think when they join a group with one of their competitors.

In reality, your competitor is either clueless and struggling, or they are already trying to adopt their own strategies. If you are marketing properly, your competitors already know what you're best at. Your road map is on your website for everyone to see; your strategic partnerships are connected to you on social media; you are proclaiming to the world your case studies from working with your best clients.

Your clueless competitors are not ones to worry about. You can out execute them even if they steal your idea if you're doing it right. Ideally you don't have low-caliber members in your Mastermind group to begin with. Higher performing competitors should have a marketing strategy that is different from yours, so they shouldn't be much of a worry either. Your company and theirs should be unique, competing on the differentiation between your company and theirs.

Michael Porter taught the business community that being the best is not a strategy. It's subjective and unsustainable. A good business owner has a strategy of differentiation from the competitors that gives you a competitive advantage over the rest. If you don't have a competitive advantage in a small group of business owners, why would you have competitive advantage once you leave the room and do business in the entire market?

Knowing that a competitor is in your Mastermind group will force you to think differently, market differently, and strategize differently. Perhaps you sell Business services to a particular industry that others do not. Maybe you deliver your service differently. Your processes could differentiate you from your competitor, or you obtain resources in a unique way. Being in a group with a competitor will force you to communicate your business in a way that makes it seem that you are in a whole different industry. That level of differentiation makes your company even more sustainable in the market.

Complimentary industries

Economic conditions that affect one industry may also affect yours in a different way or with different timing, yet still be beneficial.

The conditions that affect one industry can often affect others in different ways or at a different time. While this may seem threatening and like it would indicate adverse impacts, it can also be beneficial to your business if you are prepared for these changes and are able to take advantage of them when they do occur. You can stay informed of these changes and be ready to respond to them in a way that helps your business grow and succeed by monitoring the trends in your industry.

Companies in complimentary industries often band together, not just in hard times, but especially in hard times. They can provide what customers need in times of uncertainty and stay profitable by sharing resources and knowledge.

One example is the partnership between airlines and hotels during times of economic uncertainty. Airlines often rely on hotel bookings to fill their planes so they will help promote their travel partners to drive business to their websites and create more demand for plane tickets.

Similarly, in the technology industry, companies may form partnerships or acquire other businesses in order to access new customers. These companies often perform in different markets but are affected the same way by certain economic conditions. They do this because they know that banding operations gives them a stronger offering for their customers.

For example, imagine that you hear a concert advertised for a particular band. That band may draw a certain crowd, but they may not be able to completely fill a venue. Many venues competing in a large city weakens the market that a band must draw from. First, potential customers are only those that have the appetite and spending power to attend a concert, then, that customer has many options between other events and activities that a city may offer on any given day. The venue marketing the band wants as many people in seats as possible. It makes sense that they would schedule another band or several other bands to help draw the crowd. These other bands couldn't be from another genre. A classic rock band and a jazz band wouldn't work, but two or three classic rock bands would. Potential customers can now come to listen to multiple bands, not just one. This gives them more value and gives the venue a stronger offering, better guaranteeing a full house.

Consider what companies are in complementary industries for your business. An insurance agency may work with financial planners and real estate agents. A bookkeeping business may work alongside a tax credits company. A software company may pair with a managed IT company. Look for other companies that share your customers and would benefit from cross-promoting with you. You can better serve your customers in times of economic uncertainty and help your business continue to grow and succeed by partnering with these complementary businesses.

Dissonant industries

Sometimes, the economic conditions that adversely affect some businesses can be a source of new opportunity for your business.

One of the most important things you're taught about investing in stocks is to diversify into multiple industries or sectors. Hedge funds do this to curb against risks in any one industry. Many times, events in a particular industry may hurt the performance of that industry, but at the same time shifts the market towards a different industry.

For instance, let's say (hypothetically), that a virus outbreak creates a global pandemic. Travel is restricted, affecting the hotel and lodging industry. If this were to happen, people would find themselves stuck at home with little to do and a vacation budget they can't spend. Those people may choose to spend more on making their home more comfortable or finally getting those household projects done. This would create more spending at home improvement stores and the consumer goods industry.

In this hypothetical example, it's likely that the first people to see the shift coming were those adversely affected - the travel and lodging industries (aside from those in the medical industry). If experts in these industries had regular conversations about business and served to advise each other on upcoming tactics, the consumer goods industry would have had more time to invest in building inventory or getting new products pushed out.

***

One client saw just that in 2020. He owns a large handyman business in Dallas, Tx. He quickly increased his revenue, taking advantage of the uptick in home improvement spending. Lending to having scalable processes, he was able to hire on more contractors and support staff and put them to work in a short time. In his Mastermind, he learned about the Great Resignation that was just in the beginning stages. He knew that there would be business savvy people looking for a change in their life.

Seeing the opportunity, he used the increase in revenue to invest in a handyman school. He targeted those business professionals to buy into his franchise. He also targeted service workers that were tired of being overworked and underpaid but knew how to treat clients. He knew that while the new franchise owners could manage the business, the service workers could be a steady source of technicians. Connections in his Mastermind also allowed him to take advantage of grants that helped his students pay for the school.

Not only did he teach his students the skills needed to work on client projects, but he also taught them how to run a handyman business. He is currently growing his company exponentially because he can train franchisees that can operate in other areas.

Business owners tend to be very in tune with the industry they serve - and they should be! Success can come sooner when businesses from multiple industries gather and share what they know.

Specialized knowledge

There are many times in business that a certain specialized knowledge is needed to solve a problem. For many business owners that are too busy to network or participate in a mastermind, this means that they will continue to fail repeatedly until they get lucky. Or they might waste hours upon countless hours on the internet trying to find the solution and how it could be implemented in their company. Busy, overworked business owners know that there is an issue that needs to be solved, but they aren't sure what the solution would be. They end up reinventing the wheel when a tire shop may be right next door. For the smart business owner, they reach out to the members of their Mastermind.

* * *

Tina began growing her business after taking it over from her father. She imported and sold various plain wooden objects to arts and crafts outlets. Originally, they sold wholesale to big box stores, but she wanted to do more. Her idea to begin selling kits online through a worldwide online retailer was a hit! Not only were they still selling to the arts and crafts stores, but teachers and community groups could easily obtain quantities that they would need for their classes.

Their company had always operated through email and paperwork. Tina knew enough to convert much of this into spreadsheets that she and her team operated from. They had a different spreadsheet for each warehouse and kept track of orders on another. She created an online shared drive to share these sheets with her team so that they could update them. Gone was the problem of trying to locate paperwork or not being in the office to find information.

Still, as the orders kept rolling in, she started noticing problems with her system. Sometimes employees would forget to update the sheets or would update the wrong sheet. There was even a time when one of the sheets was accidentally deleted. Luckily, she was able to retrieve it through the file-share system. She began having a meeting with her team on Fridays where they would reconcile the sheets and her accounting books. It would nearly take the entire day. Most of the time, she spent the weekends doing this herself.

One day, Tina was having lunch with her insurance agent. The increase in warehousing needs meant that she needed to make sure she was appropriately covered. Her agent could tell that she was tired and worn out. After asking her about how the business was going, Tina told him about the problem she was having with her employees.

"They just can't keep these spreadsheets updated! It's not hard! Why can't I find good employees?" Her agent told her about a system that one of his other clients used.

"It's called an ERP", he said.

He explained how it manages orders and inventory, taking the information right from the vendors and customers. It even makes doing an inventory audit a breeze. Through his network, he was able to put her in touch with our organization. We helped her company implement a small business ERP system that saved her time and headache immediately. It also allowed for her to continue to focus on market share gaining initiatives that increased her company's revenue even more.

* * *

A good network or mastermind of business owners that you trust and know your business can help you identify gaps in your business and help you know what you don't know. Business owners that are in tune with their business and the market around them can make decisions faster, and with more accuracy. The right mastermind can help you grow your business through collaboration, sharing of knowledge, and offering new solutions to problems that arise.

The wisdom of crowds versus group think

When it comes to decision making within a business environment, the concept of 'group think' is often cited as one of the most damaging sources of errors. This phenomenon occurs when a group or organization has adopted a certain set of norms and values which heavily influence the decisions made by its members. As such, rather than being open minded and considerate to new ideas, the group is often inclined to more readily accept predetermined solutions based on established opinions and collective assumptions. On the other hand, 'wisdom of crowds' refers to an alternative approach that places more focus on coordinating thoughts from various individuals to achieve a better solution than what any single member might have produced alone.

At its core, groupthink is based on two primary principles: conformity and consensus. That is, once a particular opinion or idea has been accepted within a group, further discussion on that topic may be quickly shut down due to members having already accepted the idea as truth. Moreover, extreme pressure can also be placed upon dissenting voices who may then feel compelled not to disagree with their peers. Ultimately this leads the group into misguided decisions where individual creativity and potential are stifled by the desire for uniformity and stability amongst members.

On the other hand, wisdom of crowds offers businesses an attractive alternative which seeks to leverage collective intelligence from multiple perspectives to bring about better solutions and outcomes rather than what could have been achieved through individual efforts alone.

According to James Surowiecki (2005), wisdom of crowds works best when it involves diversity among participants regarding demographic variables such as age, gender, culture etc., cognition (knowledge) as well as opinion (perspective). Organizations can establish conditions for wise crowd behavior by ensuring that these fundamental aspects are met before beginning any decision-making process. This means that companies that are faced with a decision should make sure that the people making the decision are highly diverse. It will make sure that the solution is as unbiased as possible.

It has also been observed that even if one or two participants within a larger group are biased towards certain pre-established notions or mindsets, there still exists strong potential for successful outcomes when the wisdom of crowds are employed. While these individuals may attempt to impose their preferences onto others, they will likely find themselves overpowered by the variety of other perspectives present within the group itself thus minimizing their own personal impact on overall decision-making processes (Surowiecki, 2005). Even if some people in a group have their own ideas, wisdom from the whole group will still make a good outcome. They might try to get other people to agree with them, but there are too many different ideas in the group for one person to make the decision.

Given these characteristics it should come as no surprise that wisdom of crowds has found widespread application across many different industries ranging from finance, marketing, oil exploration, and software development, among others. Its versatility can be attributed largely due its capacity for allowing different stakeholders with diverse interests to come together so that each contributes their respective expertise towards fostering innovative ideas, leading towards greater organizational success.

The 'wisdom of crowds' offers businesses viable methods for tackling complex problems. It is important for organizations to recognize that to optimize their decision-making processes, they must embrace and continue to develop an environment within which group think is no longer the norm. Groups of people can help businesses solve difficult problems. Businesses need to stop relying on one person's opinion and start listening to many different people. This way, a lot of different kinds of people can work together to find the best solutions.

Small groups

Previously I mentioned that one of the weaknesses of a mastermind group can be that it is easy to get lost in the crowd, especially if your mastermind is larger. You may feel that other members with more seniority know what's going on and you feel less open to share and start discussions on anything. Onboarding into the mastermind can sometimes be a bit unorganized. Most don't share a welcome packet and even a new member welcome announcement may not really help that much. It's almost like showing up to a new networking group and being 2 hours late on top of that. You walk into the room and are just overwhelmed and feel like everyone else knows what's going on but you. We've all been there before.

One way to solve that problem is to form mastermind small groups within the larger group. This would be a group of less than 10 people who you can form a closer relationship with. On top of any interactions with the mastermind group, you would meet with your small group on a weekly or monthly basis.

The purpose of a mastermind small group is to make sure that you take full advantage of the power of your mastermind group. In a small group you have a more concentrated team of peers to work with. During this meeting you have a better chance to have your voice heard and be a more effective giver. You would have more time to discuss issues and potentially accomplish a task together. You may utilize your small group to work on a project from a topic that was discussed in your last mastermind group.

For instance, maybe you had a mastermind group meeting where a speaker talked about marketing materials. He may have been an expert in marketing and copy; talked about getting collateral printed and keeping it consistent with digital versions, and how and when to use that collateral.

In the small group, you may meet somewhere or online and talk about some of the ideas you got during the mastermind presentation. You may take some time during the meeting to work on your collateral or peer review someone else's collateral. Maybe somebody in the group is better at writing copy then you, but you might be better at knowing which colors to use or how the graphics should be laid out.

Another point of a mastermind small group is accountability. You have access to valuable information, but our human nature sometimes gets in the way. It's easy to get distracted in a roomful of a hundred people or more. It's also common for a person to come to the next mastermind meeting with a list of action items still not completed from the one before. If you don't take the time to utilize the value in your mastermind group, what's the point of the time and expense?

Your mastermind small group will help keep you accountable to the tasks you set yourself for in the last mastermind meeting. They may also be able to remind you about a few things that were missed when you tuned out or we're answering an important work email.

A diverse mastermind small group is exponentially valuable because the people in your group are part of the larger team. They are hearing the same experts you are hearing and can speak the same language. Yet, they also have their own diverse experiences and perspectives. Perhaps you heard a piece of advice one way, but hearing it retold from someone else from another perspective helps spark creativity in solving solutions in a new way that you may not have thought of on your own.

Some mastermind groups have structured management and may create and assign small groups for you. But what if they don't? Either officially or unofficially, create your own small group. It's usually a good idea to get the blessing from whoever is leading the main mastermind group. There may be certain values or rules that they want to make sure are carried out, but a good mastermind group would see the value in a small group and may even adopt small groups as part of their operation.

The first step is to reach out to a few members of the mastermind group. This may be members who went to a conference and joined alongside you. Maybe this is a group of people that live in the same city as you, went to the same college, or share a similar interest. Business owners in complementary industries are a great choice for a mastermind small group. Instead of helping each other work on your own tasks, you may form joint venture projects and build on those together. Whoever you choose to be in your small group, you want to make sure that they are committed to the success of the group, have a great attitude, and are givers.

The intimate nature of a small group is going to require a little more organization and process than just attending the mastermind group. There are a few suggested guidelines at the end of this chapter that you may decide to follow. These guidelines just help maintain order and retain the culture and values from your mastermind group.

Just like any other meeting, setting and communicating an agenda helps keep the meeting moving forward and being productive. The first meeting or two might focus on getting to know everyone in the group and the value that each could provide. More than the typical thirty-second introduction, you will want to start getting more familiar with each person in your group; and not only what they do professionally and what customers they are looking for. Learn what got them to where they are and what skill set they are really good at.

Once you have set a pace for your small group, you may create an agenda template. This will help members get the most out of their involvement. An example agenda is at the end of this chapter. Spend the first few minutes going around the group to talk about any news that has come up in their life or business and an issue that they are currently working through. Don't stop to talk about these just yet but take good notes so that your group can come back to it.

Once everyone is warmed up, shift the focus to recap your last mastermind group meeting. Let members talk about what stuck out to them the most and what sort of action they felt led to take. Take note of some of the questions that members might have had or aspects they may not have been clear on. Perhaps others had a different take on the subject. Does the clarification help any issues that a member brought up in the first ten minutes? Or are new questions raised? If so, can you solve this as a group?

In the next 3 sections, focus the group on one particular issue raised. Spend 10 to 15 minutes discovering the root of the issue and how it may be solved. If you all agreed to a working session, with named deliverables by the end of the meeting, you may spend even more time on each issue.

End the meeting by listing any follow up activities that need to happen. Did an issue not get completely resolved? Are there deeper questions that should go to the main mastermind? Are there any one on ones that may need to happen between group members? It's a good idea to document these in a follow-up email to the group.

Your mastermind small group will need someone to lead and coordinate the group. You can assign leadership in a semi-permanent fashion, or trade leadership responsibilities each month or so. The leader would be responsible for scheduling the small group meetings, setting up the venue, and making sure that the agenda and culture is upheld.

Mastermind Code of Conduct

1. Small group members recognize the value of meeting consistently. Any member who misses two meetings in a row may be subject to dismissal from the small group.

2. Small group members will abide by the same rules, guidelines, and code of conduct as The Mastermind group.

3. Small group members will act in a manner of polite discourse when discussing topics.

4. At all times, members must exhibit the utmost standards of professional conduct when collaborating and communicating with one another. This means conducting themselves honorably, fairly, and in good faith at any time within this membership community — past, present, or future.

5. It is expected that members will make a concerted effort to arrive on time and minimize any disturbances when they have accepted an agreed upon meeting time.

6. Members should actively strive to reduce the spread of misinformation by using only well-informed opinions in any communication.

7. Members should only accept responsibilities they are both capable of and willing to fulfill. When it is no longer possible for them to live up to their commitments, members must reach out for assistance or seek a release from duty.

8. Our varied perspectives in the workplace push us to think outside of our comfort zones, permitting us to be more imaginative and inventive in the services we provide. We understand that the world is composed of different social customs and cultural backgrounds, so we honor these distinctions with respect.

9. As a key part of healthy communication, members of the organization must exhibit courtesy, etiquette, and politeness to all those inside or outside their group. It is essential for everyone involved to act respectfully toward one another.

10. Maintain a culture of good manners, civility, and respect at work. We encourage everyone to create an atmosphere rooted in positivity and don't hesitate to voice their concerns when this is not followed through by any team member.

Small group agenda example:

10 min (1 min ea.) - around the table updates
15 min - perspectives and takeaways
15 min - Issue #1
15 min - Issue #2
15 min - Issue #3
10 min - follow-up activities

***

Overall, mentors and mastermind groups both have their strengths and weaknesses. Mentors are great for providing individualized advice while mastermind groups can offer a diverse range of perspectives from multiple experts in different industries. When it comes to making decisions or solving problems related to your business, having access to the wisdom of crowds is invaluable. Ultimately, the decision on whether you should choose a mentor or join a mastermind group will depend on how much time and effort you want to invest into developing relationships with others who may be able to help guide your path towards success as an entrepreneur. No matter which routes you take, make sure that it's something that aligns with your goals as well as provides support when needed so that you can achieve success in all aspects of life!

Wisdom of an Advisory Board

Advisory boards are an invaluable asset to any business or organization. An advisory board allows for more informed decision-making that benefits the entire organization by drawing on the experience and expertise of a diverse group of individuals.

At its core, an advisory board is composed of individuals who have a vested interest in the success of the organization and an understanding of how various aspects of it work. This may include industry leaders, figures from within the organization itself, entrepreneurs with relevant experience, or other professionals with specialized knowledge. In some cases, advisory boards are made up exclusively of members external to the organization.

Experienced board of advisors

When assembling an advisory board, it is important to consider the different types of expertise and experience required. A well-rounded board should have a combination of industry veterans, financial experts, sales and marketing professionals, legal advisors, and other subject matter experts. There may be specific areas such as technology or regulatory requirements that should also be represented, depending on the business.

One important role of an advisory board is to provide objective, unbiased advice and feedback on the business plan and other decisions. The board can also serve as a sounding board for new ideas or initiatives, helping you identify potential risks or opportunities early on. In addition, they may be able to connect you with additional resources or networking opportunities that can help drive growth.

If you are looking to assemble an advisory board for your business, start by identifying and recruiting the right candidates. Look in your own network first and reach out to respected professionals who have experience in the industry or sector of your business. Once you have a solid foundation of advisors, build upon it over time with additional experts as the needs of your business change. You can be confident that you have access to invaluable knowledge and experience to help your business thrive with the right advisory board in place.

Meeting with your board of advisors is an incredibly important part of running a successful business. As such, it is critical that meetings with the board are well-planned and structured, with clearly defined roles and expectations. It is also important to ensure that there is an appropriate level of involvement on the part of your advisors. While you should welcome their input and feedback, it is ultimately your decision whether or not to act upon it.

It is important to assemble the right team and involve them in decision-making, it's also essential not to be afraid to ask for their help. Schedule regular meetings with your board and make sure that you cover the entire breadth of your company. Be open, honest, and transparent with your board members. Trust and respect are key to building a successful relationship with your advisors.

In addition to providing valuable insight into your business, board meetings can also be a great opportunity to network and build relationships with other business leaders. This can help you develop new professional contacts, gain additional expertise, or find potential partners or investors for your business.

Skeletons in the closet

Your business isn't perfect. No business is. Oftentimes, I have seen clients that are afraid to start working with advisors because they feel that their business isn't ready for it yet. That's like not bringing in a home remodeler because you have a sink full of dishes. It's just not practical. Your board of advisors can be an invaluable resource, but only if you are open and honest with them about the state of your business. If you have any skeletons in the closet, or if there are any issues that may make building your business difficult, don't be afraid to discuss them with your advisors. They can help you navigate those challenges and provide guidance on how to overcome them.

If you are holding back something that is illegal or suspicious, that is something you definitely need to address. It may even be something like not being completely forthcoming on your taxes. Think back to your mission statement and your values. Hopefully any situation like this goes against your values and mission statement. Be honest with yourself. This is the time to fix your business so that you can move forward. If you need help, reach out and get it. It will be much better to address this sooner than later.

Other skeletons may be just some dirty housekeeping. Don't worry about that. Trust me, your advisors have seen worse and understand that you are reaching out for our help. You trust your advisory board and they trust that you will follow their advice and clean your business up. There's no judgment here. You're all in this together to move forward.

Providing data

It's important to give your advisory board concise data on your business. You are relying on them for their advice and experience. Don't give them homework that will make them dig for information or give them incomplete data that doesn't give them a complete big picture of the status of your company. Key performance indicators, Gap issues, and recent progress are all important topics to cover with your board. If you've implemented these from previous chapters, it should be an easy meeting to hold.

At the end of your meeting, you may feel that you have more questions than answers. That's ok! Your board members are there to help you, so don't be afraid to ask questions or seek input as needed. Remember that a successful relationship with your board will only benefit your business. So be open, trust your advisors, and work together to build a stronger and more successful company.

It is essential for businesses to assemble a board of advisors who can provide valuable insight into their operations, as well as network and build relationships with other business leaders. If you are facing challenges in your business or have skeletons in the closet, be honest and open with your board members so that they can offer guidance and support to help you move forward. Additionally, it is important to gather and provide clear data on key performance indicators so that your board members can provide targeted, actionable advice. With the help of your board of advisors, you can build a stronger and more successful business!

Taking advice

As I conversed with Brenda at the networking event, we made polite conversation before delving further into what our professions entailed. She described her search for resources, and it was then that I revealed my calling as a consultant aiding businesses to identify such sources. She was looking for somebody to build a website and needed to get funding.

"Funding for a website?", I asked. "I'm not sure that VC or angel funding would be the way to go just to create a website."

I explained to her that you can get a decent website for around $10,000. With a little bit of web surfing and tutorials, you can even throw one up yourself. This prompted us to arrange a formal meeting.
Our mission was to understand her requirements, and I could see she was struggling to express herself. I scheduled a conversation with her, myself, and two other people. I invited an individual who specialized in building cost-effective websites, and another representative from a promotional organization. Brenda explained her concept to our team, and it quickly became apparent that we weren't dealing with a website but rather, an internet-based web application. This cutting-edge program would provide users the capability to easily search through pertinent market information, manipulate data, generate graphs, and analyze maps all in one place. We were thrilled as soon as she began describing this opportunity! This information could not only benefit those who are in

the market for that product, but it would also be beneficial to manufacturers who can provide consumers with a wealth of useful knowledge. This truly seemed like an excellent concept.

After scouring the internet for years and coming up empty-handed, Brenda believed that a website like this one didn't exist - even in today's digital age. She had an intimate knowledge of both consumers and suppliers due to her industry experience, as well as a burning passion for what she wanted to create. This made it almost impossible for her not to launch this business!

Despite having no proof of concept or strategy, Brenda had already approached two web development companies for quotes to build a website. I realized that either they were taking advantage of her lack of understanding regarding the idea she was pursuing, or equally concerning - simply didn't comprehend it themselves.

Would this be a subscription service? Would this be free with paid advertisements? Where would all this vast amount of data come from? She was oblivious to any of these answers. But the website companies promised her that they'd create a website if she supplied them with the data. I don't think it even crossed their minds that this was an intricate web application.

I was elated to have the opportunity of making her vision come true, so I offered my consulting services at a discounted rate. After all, she's investing her hard-earned savings and I wanted to make sure that each penny is wisely spent - without wasting time or resources on expensive proof-of-concepts before we knew that the idea was truly viable. To help Brenda accomplish her goal, I recommended that we start by conducting a SWOT analysis to identify and anticipate both internal strengths and weaknesses as well as external opportunities and threats. Additionally, it was imperative for us to document the application's requirements for us to design the minimum viable product (MVP).

We convened at our workplace, and she presented an abundant binder full of web page printouts, illustrations, brochures, and a plethora of data on the market. Apparently, someone had done some research for her several years ago. She believed that this was it - finally she'd create this company and sell it off for huge profit before retiring comfortably. And even if all her savings were spent on the venture it would be worth every penny!

We set out to pinpoint the strengths and weaknesses of her startup business. Despite there not being too many clear-cut strong points, she was well versed in her industry which gave us something positive to work with. We filled in all that we could regarding potential opportunities and threats. We then took out another whiteboard and brainstormed who our users would be, as well as what information they required in order to make decisions. We discussed how we could potentially access the data needed for these consumers. Additionally, we devoted some time to thinking of ways that this data can be obtained.

After adjournment, I advised that we take the time in between meetings to conduct further market research. She seemed satisfied with this, yet her main desire was for us to move forward and begin creating a business plan. She suggested our next step should be procuring data from suppliers so that we could get started building the website.

Before I even arrived home, Brenda had sent me several emails with a variety of vendors and websites for us to contact in order to find the data she thought we should be looking for. In response, I reminded her that we still had a few more steps to go before getting started. However, I reassured her that conducting market research was the most important step to make sure her idea was viable and worth investing in. She graciously agreed with me and allowed us to pursue further exploration into the concept.

After organizing our meeting minutes, we began doing some early-stage market research. I considered if I were an end user who was interested in buying the product - what would I type into a search bar? After entering my query and pressing enter, the results appeared on screen.

The first link in the results pointed to her biggest rival. When I examined their website, it became evident that my client was right - they were providing info about a product of a similar nature but weren't targeting precisely the same market segment as she intended to appeal to. Nevertheless, this posed a significant warning and could potentially be an obstacle to establishing her company. I conducted an extensive investigation into this competitor to uncover the scope of their expenses and understand where they were headed in terms of market share. Amazingly, I discovered that their marketing spend alone cost them billions of dollars. This posed a major issue; if my client's web application required $300,000 or $500,000 just to enter the market – how easy would it be for her competition to observe what she's doing and incorporate similar ideas within their system?

With the right move, these competitors could quickly gain an edge on her. I brainstormed a way to give her an upper hand. If she developed and sold some proprietary technology that allowed them to access and use this data efficiently, then maybe they'd have no choice but to buy it from her. Refocusing my attention back on the task at hand, I resumed trawling through search results.

As I continued clicking through links, I stumbled across a website that was completely unfamiliar to me. Upon further inspection, it seemed like this platform had practically everything Brenda wanted — it fulfilled each and every one of her requirements!

Needless to say, my initial shock quickly turned into disappointment. There wasn't anything unique or new here that she hadn't already requested. It appears all the work has been done for us - but unfortunately without any room left for creativity.

I wondered if she simply hasn't searched for competitors recently. Or perhaps I misinterpreted the specifications or maybe something was left out of consideration. After further investigation into this website, it became evident that 15 years ago someone purchased the domain name and for at least 10 years, it had been quite unattractive with little activity and limited content available. But five years back there was a plethora of improvements made to its design - several things we discussed during our strategy session were already incorporated within the site! The website had referrals to accessory sites, a paid subscription option and educational blogs on the market. As soon as I saw it, I knew that if I was looking for this product or service, then this is the destination site!

It puzzled me why no one else seemed to be aware of its existence. With a feeling of dread, I picked up the phone and dialed her number the following day, bracing myself for an uncomfortable conversation.

"Brenda... I just wanted to know if maybe I understood all the requirements for this product. Or perhaps if you had done any research into the market anytime recently?", I asked her.

After she confessed it had been a while since she'd glanced at the competition, I suggested her visit her competitor's website. As soon as I showed how the features that were discussed fit perfectly, what she said next amazed me beyond belief! She knew about the website!

We spent hours in a conference room already, talking about the uniqueness of her idea and she knew this website was out there?!

"Yeah", she said, "But how are they getting the data? If they got it, we could get it."

I paused. I don't think she really understood. "But Brenda, your idea already exists. It took them 15 years to get there. Even then, the analytics show that not many people even visit this website. No one even knows about it. If we compare traffic of this website to the larger competitor, it doesn't even show up on the graph."

"I don't want to talk about that competitor.", She said. "They don't do what I want to offer. I don't understand why we're even mentioning them."

"Yes, I know that they aren't in the same exact market, but everyone knows about this competitor. They go to this competitor if they even have an inkling of an interest and have an internet connection. If they want any information on this market, this is where they're going to go. It doesn't matter if it's not accurate information. Even if it's not full information. This is what they know."

Again, she exclaimed it. "Doesn't matter. I don't want to talk about that company. That company is not the website that I want to create. We need to figure out how that other company got the data and build our own website."

I was stuck. It seemed so clear-cut, but I couldn't make her understand.

***

Having a vision for one's company is essential, as is maintaining enthusiasm and passion for it. However, too often entrepreneurs get too attached to their business that they don't want to hear anything negative about it - regardless of data or professional advice. No matter how much evidence there may be in favor of the argument presented by another party, hearing out criticism might not always be on top of an owner's list when protecting their business interests are concerned. Staying open to criticism and acting on it can be key to a business's success.

It is important to remember that those who are offering critiques or advice did not create the company; they are simply trying to help an entrepreneur find ways to make their business more successful. As such, taking the time to listen and consider what has been said can result in new ideas or strategies for growth. Additionally, hearing out criticisms does not mean automatically succumbing to them - owners should still have full control over the direction of their business. What is important is that entrepreneurs take all feedback into consideration when making decisions about their operations.

* * *

Businesses that succeed do so because their owners have taken the opportunity to evolve with changing times. This means staying open to criticism and acting on it when appropriate. Entrepreneurs can gain valuable insights into what works and what doesn't by actively listening to others. It allows them to make the necessary adjustments needed for success.

It is essential to assemble an advisory board that has a diverse range of expertise and experience. This will ensure that any decision-making process is well informed and beneficial for the organization as a whole. Furthermore, it is important to be open with your advisors about challenges or issues you may have to get the most out of their advice. Lastly, provide them with concise data on your business so they can give accurate guidance based on facts rather than assumptions.

Ultimately, being open to constructive criticism is essential for any company that wants to stay competitive and remain successful in a rapidly changing marketplace.

George Mayfield

"You are who you build yourself to be."

— *Francis Shenstone, The Explorer's Mindset: Unlock Health Happiness and Success the Fun Way*

Recharge and Refocus

It is essential for executives to periodically step away from their day-to-day work and recharge to maintain a high level of productivity and efficiency. There are many important reasons for businesses to take the time for executive retreats, strategic workshops, and executive wellness. This allows them to come back with a fresh perspective and renewed energy. Additionally, by taking the time for strategic workshops, businesses can focus on specific goals and objectives and create a plan of action to achieve them. Executive wellness is also critical as it helps keep executives healthy both physically and mentally, which in turn benefits the business as a whole.

As a business executive, I have found that taking the time for executive retreats, strategic workshops, and executive wellness is one of the most important things I can do to keep my business running smoothly and efficiently. These activities help me recharge and refocus when I need it the most, allowing me to come back with a renewed sense of purpose and energy. They also give me the opportunity to focus on specific goals for my business and create an action plan to achieve them.

Additionally, executive wellness is an essential component of running a successful business. By taking steps to stay physically and mentally healthy, I can be at my best and make better decisions for my company. Whether it's taking a walk during lunch to clear my head or finding time for meditation in the evening, I know that these small measures can have a big impact on my overall well-being and success.

Executive retreats

Executive retreats are a way for business leaders to take some time out of the office and focus on their company strategy, mindset, and health. They usually involve a few days of intensive work and team building, followed by some relaxation time. The goal is to come up with new ideas and strategies, and to recharge and refocus. It's common to see executives at large corporations taking the time and expense to go on a team retreat, but much less common to see entrepreneurs and smaller teams taking the time to do the same.

It can be difficult to justify the cost and time away from work for a retreat if you're an entrepreneur or small business owner. But there are several benefits to taking the time for executive retreats, including:

1. Clearer strategic thinking. Spending time in a distraction-free environment allows you to focus on your work and refine your business strategy.

2. Fresh perspectives. Being around a group of people with a variety of backgrounds and experiences can help uncover new ideas and approaches to problems.

3. Building team cohesion. Spending time together outside of the office can help build stronger relationships and foster a sense of team spirit.

4. Increased productivity. When you return to the office, you'll be motivated and energized – ready to take on your work with new enthusiasm.

If you're considering an executive retreat for your business, there are a few things to keep in mind. First, it's important to find the right location and setting – one that is distraction-free and allows you to focus on your work. They can be done onsite or offsite. Onsite is more cost effective, but offsite can be just as distracting (if not moreso, especially if there's attractions beckoning your attention). The important thing is to stay focused on your objectives. So, if you do choose an onsite workshop, make sure your managers know to keep distractions from reaching those involved. If you do an offsite meeting, no golf until you're done!

You should also make sure that the retreat is well-organized, with clear goals and a well-defined schedule. Don't try to cram too much into too little time. Schedule down time for mental breaks and to stretch your legs. And, of course, don't forget to bring plenty of snacks and refreshments – you'll need all the energy you can get!

Finally, it's important to plan for after the retreat – ensuring that you have clear follow-up processes in place to capture and act on the ideas that come out of it. Documenting the results of the retreat and assigning accountability will ensure that the effort was worth the time and expense. With these considerations in mind, an executive retreat can be a valuable tool for entrepreneurs.

Strategic workshops

Previously, you read about strategic exercises like value chain analysis (your company machine) and SWOT. Executive retreats are good opportunities to refresh these models and develop the budgets for your company and departments, but you don't have to wait for a retreat to put them on.

It's a common occurrence in my consulting practice to have to really do some convincing the first time we do a workshop. Business owners have been down in the weeds working for so long that stopping work and planning ahead seems like a foreign idea. Working feels like work and "sitting around in a conference room all day" seems like a waste of time. "We're too busy for a strategic workshop", they'd say. As you know by now, being busy may have gotten you to the point you are, but it won't let you grow. You can't scale busy.

A SWOT or Value Chain analysis will help you figure out what gaps you need to fill and give you a good starting point to develop your strategy. There may be other workshops that you would find value in depending on your current needs and where your company is.

Vision Board - A vision board is a tool used to spark your creativity and motivate you to create the business that you want. It's a fun, visual way to manifest your dreams and goals by putting them up in plain sight. The idea behind creating a vision board is simple: you cut out pictures from magazines and other sources that represent your goals, dreams, and aspirations. You then paste them onto a board to create a collage that displays your vision for the future. Involving the whole leadership team can be a fun, yet eye opening experience.

Culture - Are you actively cultivating the culture you want for your business? Do you even know what the best culture would serve your business and its customers best? Strategically thinking about what your company culture is and where it needs to be will help you create a company that people want to work for, and customers enjoy doing business with. Consider your company's mission and come up with 3 - 5 values that would serve you best. Examples are integrity, quality, and customer centricity. Make sure that they can be used to help people make decisions and that they can serve you for years to come. Brainstorm ways you can bring those values to life in your business.

Enhance Team Collaboration - This workshop would focus on teaching effective methods of collaboration between members of the executive team, as well as between the executives and their subordinates. One of the most important factors for business success is collaboration, but that doesn't always come naturally. By learning how to properly communicate and work together as a team, your company will be able to accomplish more goals and be more productive. The workshop could include team building activities such as escape rooms, puzzle challenges, or other fun and engaging games that encourage teamwork and communication.

Social Media Challenge - Are you and your employees' social media accounts serving each other and your business? Having a workshop that teaches people how to supercharge their accounts will help them professionally and, in turn, boost your company. Posting etiquette, Profile do's and don'ts, and recommendation writing, among other things would quickly enhance the value of your team. When outsiders view you and your employee's profiles, they will know that you hire quality people. Prepare by having a graphic artist make a portfolio of banners, logos, and other art organized by social media platform. Having a photographer ready to take fresh headshots as well as action shots of your workshop can enhance the value of your time.

Employee Onboarding - Taking the time to get perspectives from your team on the weaknesses of your current employee onboarding program can help your employees find success and engage with your team quickly. Create an onboarding presentation from your leadership team that lets your new employees know that you welcome and appreciate their skills and what they can add to your team. Describing your values and why they are important gives them a clear understanding of what's expected. Don't forget to include employee perspective and buy-in (and that you practice what you preach) before you push it out to the company. The last thing you want is new employees thinking that your leadership team is self-serving.

Including workshops in your company activities is a good way to quickly get something major done. The investment should be lasting and should be able to pay for itself relatively quickly. If you want your company to reach its full potential, adding unique workshops to the agenda of your event is a great way to start. From improving company culture to employee onboarding, your retreat can be tailored to your team's needs. By ensuring that every step is carefully planned and executed, you can get real value out of the experience.

Wellness

Company leaders have a critical role in setting the tone and foundation for any organization. It is essential to prioritize wellness for company leaders to ensure that the organization is successful and productive. Focusing on wellness can help senior management reduce stress levels, increase energy, promote better decision making, and drive better results from their teams. Wellness is an important priority for company leaders, as it has a direct impact on their ability to succeed. At the core of wellness is reducing stress and increasing energy levels, both of which are vital for senior management in making good decisions and driving productivity from their teams.

Get enough sleep - One of the most important things you can do for your health is to get enough sleep. Most adults need between 7 and 8 hours of sleep per night. Far too often, I hear business leaders talk about getting only 4 hours of sleep most nights. Oftentimes, it's said like a badge they wear proudly on their chest. Getting enough sleep can help improve your mood, increase your energy level, and reduce your risk of developing chronic health problems. Lack of proper sleep can affect your decision-making abilities, especially in a crisis. Recent research has shown a strong correlation between lack of sleep and the onset of schizophrenia-like symptoms, such as hallucinations and disorganized behavior.

Eat a healthy diet - Another important aspect of maintaining your health is to eat a healthy diet. Eating plenty of fruits, vegetables, and whole grains can help reduce your risk of developing heart disease, stroke, and diabetes. Additionally, eating a healthy diet can help you maintain a healthy weight, which is important for reducing your risk of developing these chronic diseases. Just like putting bad gas in your car, eating bad food can have both immediate and lasting effects. Consult your doctor to make the best decisions on the right diet for you. Even a good diet can be bad if implemented incorrectly.

Exercise regularly - Exercising regularly is another key component of maintaining your health. Exercise can help reduce your risk of developing chronic diseases such as heart disease, stroke, and diabetes. Additionally, exercise can help you maintain a healthy weight, which is important for reducing your risk of developing these chronic diseases. Many times, I have implemented a "walking meeting policy" with my teams. When appropriate, we take our meeting outside and walk around the block. There is still an agenda and it's still important to focus on the topic, but a walking meeting can help give you and your team the ability to exercise and be productive at the same time. This is especially helpful for meetings where you are solving a problem creatively.

Reduce stress - Stress can have a negative impact on your health, so it's important to find ways to reduce stress in your life. There are many ways to reduce stress, such as meditation, yoga, and quiet reading. Many times, I have found that the best way to reduce stress is to simply take some time off and unplug. Whether you go on a weekend trip, or just sit in front of the TV at home, making time for yourself is critical to reducing stress and restoring your energy. Balance is key in finding the method that works best for you.

Retrain your Brain - Your brain is evolving, flexible, and restorable. Retraining your brain gets rid of bad habits like inattentiveness and attempting to multitask. It can help you to recall details and problem solve quickly. It can help you fight the possibility of mental disease, depression, and the long-term effects of stress. I urge you to find out more from experts like those at the Center for Brain Health (www.centerforbrainhealth.org), who offers education and workshops for individuals and groups.

See your doctor regularly - Finally, it's important to see your doctor regularly for checkups. Seeing your doctor on a regular basis can help identify any potential health problems early on so that they can be treated before they become serious.

Overall, focusing on wellness for company leaders is critical for ensuring that the organization is operating at its best. Leaders can set the tone for a positive and productive workplace culture by prioritizing things like mindfulness meditation, exercise, healthy eating, and regular sleep. Ultimately, this will benefit both employees and the organization by creating an environment that fosters success and growth.

* * *

Overall, executive retreats are an important tool for business leaders to take time out of the office and focus on their company strategy, mindset, and health. Additionally, executives must prioritize wellness to ensure that their organization is successful and productive. When senior management reduces stress levels and increases energy, they can make better decisions which lead to greater productivity from their teams. Executives can maintain a healthy balance between work life and personal life while still driving positive results for themselves and their businesses by taking regular breaks away from work or participating in activities such as meditation or exercise. With these tips in mind, you should be well-equipped to create a culture of wellness within your team that will help drive success in all aspects of your business operations.

George Mayfield

All Boats Rise with the Tide

When the tide rises, all boats rise with it. This fundamental truth is evident in many facets of our lives, from business to relationships. There's no limit to what we can achieve together when we are surrounded by a supportive, vibrant community that celebrates success. We enjoy a shared prosperity - where each of us can contribute something meaningful or special to the group and be duly rewarded for that contribution. Consequently, it pays off for everyone when we put aside our differences and share our successes. Working collaboratively together to lift each other up is ultimately far more rewarding than working against one another or competing against ourselves. We can create something truly great by recognizing the power of collective action.

Flow power to power

The best way to grow your business and your brand is to position yourself as a conduit between others. Success is a sort of energy that flows in the world freely. You can't simply reach out and harness it yourself; you must let it flow through you and direct it towards others. I know it seems counter intuitive to share success with others when you're trying to be as successful as you can, but sharing your wins, your relationships, your expertise with others will reward you over and over.

A friend of mine, Ken Walls, once told me how he grew his business from nearly nothing to a continuously successful consulting company. He targeted well-known people in his industry. People he wanted to do business with and people who had clients that he knew he could help. He became that person's number one fan, getting on social media and telling everyone he could how great that person's product was. He went so far as to give out gift cards to people who could answer questions from his target's book. Before long, he got that person's attention in a big way. It changed his business and life. It changed the lives of so many others that he's affected.

He didn't stop there. He continues to give his knowledge and share his expertise with those willing to do the work. Now, he calls many people with wealth and resources close friends, but he shares that generosity, lifting others up to his level and serving his community. Look up Ken Walls to hear more about his story.

bit.ly/FWKenWalls

Sure, you can target celebrities, and that might work, but you should start with those close to you. Likely, there are already other business owners you know. You network with them, you work with them, you might share hobbies with them. Everyone has a need. To flow power to them, get to know what their needs are, especially if it's not a need you fill. This isn't about you. Find others in your network that you can introduce them to. Do more than a lazy email. Bringing steel and flint to a pile of wood doesn't make a fire. They need to know why you thought they should know each other. You need to be the spark that ignites the conversation that they need.

Avoid common generic tropes like "you guys work in similar spaces", and "I think there might be some overlap", or the worst of them all, "John, meet Susan. I'll let you take it from here.". All you're doing is assigning homework and no one likes that! If you do that enough times (maybe even just once), you'll see that person distance themselves from you, I promise.

A good template I often use is to treat each person like they are both valued guests on a show. Make them feel like the relationship we already share is special (and it is). Each person gets an introduction of a few sentences on what makes them great. It shows them that I truly do value them in my network and that I've been paying attention. I know who they are, remember the conversations we've had, and even know some of the recent successes they might have shared online. The other guest also sees that I value that other person's connection. They also know more about them than they can glean from an email domain.

I, then, write about how I believe they may be able to help each other. Perhaps there's a specific client that one has that could use some help outside of their offering. Maybe there's a project one has been talking about that could use some collaboration. Maybe there's even a shared hobby.

I end the email by including relevant links to them both; be it their website or social media profile. Make it easy for them to find out more before responding. Remember, your job is to make each of your guests excited about meeting each other.

If you can spark action between two or more people, you will find that they will come to value you in their network. You will be rewarded over and over if you are genuine.

Being part of something bigger

In business and in life, you must be part of something bigger than yourself. This concept applies to business owners and business leaders because focusing solely on your own company can limit growth potential.

Being part of something bigger provides opportunities for growth that may otherwise not be available. Working with other companies or organizations opens new doors and allows you to explore different markets and customer bases, which can lead to increased revenue and greater success. It also gives you the chance to gain access to resources such as talent pools, technology, and capital that may be out of reach when operating independently.

Collaborating with other organizations also opens the possibility for creative solutions that one individual or organization might not have thought of on their own. By working together, businesses can pool their resources and knowledge to come up with innovative ideas that could propel them further than they could have gone alone. This could result in new products or services that would appeal to customers more effectively than what you already offer.

Partnering with other brands or businesses can help increase your brand recognition by exposing you to a larger audience outside your existing customer base. Aligning yourself with strong players within and outside of your industry can also lend credibility to your brand, which is important for building trust among current and potential customers alike. Additionally, it gives your business an opportunity to create relationships with other influencers who may be able to provide valuable advice on how best to promote your brand or products.

Being part of something bigger rather than just focusing on your own company has numerous benefits for both small businesses and large corporations alike. Opportunities for growth are opened when working together, collaboration leads to creative solutions, and brand recognition is improved when partnering with influential players in the industry. All these factors combine into a powerful strategy that helps businesses succeed in today's competitive market environment.

Businesses flourish when you put aside selfish needs. Don't be afraid to put aside your pride, focus on others, and share the love. You'll find that when you lift others up and other businesses, they will return the favor tenfold. Your business and brand will grow as a result, and it all starts with sharing success instead of hoarding it like a miser. Together, we can all power our way to the top.

Creating shared value

Shared value is a unique principle wherein businesses can increase their profits while simultaneously making the world around them better. Unlike philanthropy, corporate social responsibility or even sustainability, shared value offers companies an opportunity to do well and do good all at once. It works by creating a win-win situation where business success contributes to social progress. This creates value for both shareholders and society, making it an important concept for any entrepreneur or business leader. Companies that embrace shared value are more likely to enjoy higher profits, increased customer loyalty and better brand reputation—all of which can lead to greater long-term success. Additionally, when businesses benefit from shared value initiatives, the effects ripple outward, improving the lives of individuals in our communities and beyond. We can all work together to build a brighter future by recognizing that profitability and social responsibility go hand in hand.

In the article, "Creating Shared Value", published in the Harvard Business Review (January-February 2011), Michael Porter and Mark Kramer explain the difference in redistributing value versus creating shared value. The goal of fair-trade coffee is to pay coffee farmers more for the same amount of coffee. While this seems like the right thing to do, it has ripple effects on the market. The price of coffee goes up without the typical causes from a competitive market. The quality of the coffee is not improved and may even decrease as companies attempt to keep the price low. Farmers are now paid more for the coffee, but there is no competitive reason to improve their crops, processes, and techniques. In a shared value model, however, companies that help to invest in the local farmer's businesses, communities, and suppliers can see drastically more improvements in production. Moreover, not just the farmers themselves, but the entire communities typically see a greater quality of life from those investments, many times over the effects of simply paying more for the coffee beans.

Addressing societal needs is an effective way for companies to become more productive. For instance, providing education programs not only improves the quality of future employees and their families but also increases overall productivity in their work. As illustrated in the accompanying graphic, there are numerous strong links between social responsibility initiatives and business results.

Harvard Business School, 2022. https://www.isc.hbs.edu/creating-shared-value/csv-explained/Pages/default.aspx

Taking this same concept to business relationships, companies that work together to build each other up can provide shared value to each other and to the business community. This offers a ripple effect of increased value to its customers, their families, and to the communities where they live.

* * *

Nick Ogilvie has seen great success in his company in the first 16 years. As an artificial turf installer, he saw the need for synthetic grass as water shortages and traditional grass expenses grew more and more. As his company became more profitable, he decided to help others in the industry. He invested in a program to help other new and existing entrepreneurs get into the artificial turf industry and has published a book on the subject. Nick works with landscapers and construction companies to invest in tools, processes, and education to offer their own turf installation services and take advantage of the increasing need for the product. But why would a business owner purposefully create competition in the marketplace?

"The need is so great", Nick says.

Nick turns away business so often that he sought to bring other companies into the market. The effect on those businesses he helps has an almost immediate positive impact on their revenue. It helps those business owners provide for their family and their employees, and it helps those companies invest in their communities in turn. The more facilities and homes that turn to high-quality artificial turf make a positive impact on society.

> *"A 1,000 to 1,500 square foot lawn consumes around 12,000 gallons of water per year. With water going up in price and becoming more scarce, the artificial turf industry is helping to save water, money, and the environment."*
> *(www.luxeblades.com)*

The shared value model of doing business has a vastly greater effect than simply redistributing profits. Companies that care enough to invest in each other, as well as their customers, employees, and local communities have far greater success than those that do not. Companies must be willing to invest in each other and look for lasting solutions that will bring about long-term success to truly benefit from the positive effects of shared value. The potential for even greater success is unlocked when we recognize that everyone is interconnected.

It is important to identify what you want to achieve and how it will help create value for both your company and the world to make sure you're reaping the most benefits from your shared value initiatives. Set ambitious goals, measure progress, and look for ways to continually improve your shared value efforts. It's also important to communicate your objectives clearly so that stakeholders understand why you're investing in shared value initiatives and how they'll benefit from them. Above all, remember that shared value is an ongoing journey—one that should be embraced with a commitment to continuous learning, adaptation, and improvement. By staying focused on long-term results, you can ensure that everyone benefits when it comes to creating shared value.

***

It's clear that working together and leveraging shared value is essential for success in business. Businesses can all benefit from each other's successes - both directly and indirectly by recognizing our interconnectedness. This approach not only increases profits but also creates a better world around us by improving lives in our communities. We can create something truly great when embracing this concept of collective action. It may sound counterintuitive to share your wins with others when you're trying to be as successful as possible, but sharing what you have will reward you over time. So don't forget: When the tide rises, all boats rise with it!

George Mayfield

"Every company needs an exit strategy and an exit plan. Ideally, the exit strategy should be agreed upon by the founders before the first dollar of investment goes into the company."

— Basil Peters, Early Exits: Exit Strategies for Entrepreneurs and Angel Investors

Find Your Exit

There is one piece of advice that I have given to people, probably more than any other. The very next thing you should do after creating a plan is to create an exit plan. You need to know ahead of time when and how you will exit if things don't go as planned. This approach helps you to be prepared for anything that may come your way in life, and it also allows you to make changes quickly if needed. It is important to have an escape route if things don't turn out the way you expect. It may seem counterintuitive, but if you have a plan in place, then you will be more likely to succeed than if you didn't prepare for the worst.

You also need to have an idea in mind for when you will want to exit if things are going as planned. You may decide that you want to stay in a certain position or situation for a while and build on it, but you should also have an idea of when the time is right to move on to something different. This allows you to maximize your potential and take advantage of opportunities as they arise. Having an exit plan gives you more control over your life and career and makes it easier to adapt to changing conditions.

Not only is this applicable to business owners and leaders, but also to people who have gotten a new job or started anything new. Even when picking up a new hobby, a person should not only know where they intend to go with it, but how long they may think they will be driven to persist with this pastime. You might find that notion ridiculous. After all, it's just a hobby. Do it until you no longer have the desire anymore, right? Well, yes - yet let me share an extreme example: Do you envision yourself still engaging in this activity when reaching your 60th or 80th birthday? Or is this something that could easily fizzle out after a season?

Setting at least a tentative end in place helps you make better decisions involving that hobby. How much money are you going to spend on equipment? Do you really need equipment that is going to last, or do you just need a beginners set? Should you pay for lessons or just wing it?

How many people do you know that started up a new sport and spent thousands of dollars for specialty clothing and equipment only for it to just sit in the closet after that first year? Of course, there's other considerations involved that might have led to that situation, like staying committed, having support, and unexpected life events that might get in the way, but if you're starting out on something new and aren't sure where you're going with it, why waste the resources?

Now, a business is much more of an investment than a hobby, but hopefully this helps illustrate the importance. You should know where you're going with your business, how long you plan to stay committed to the strategy, and how you should exit whether things are going well or poorly.

* * *

One of my good friends, Dagmar Metzler, was recently telling me about her father and some of the things he taught her growing up. He was ex-military intelligence and was a bit cynical about trusting strangers and was very adamant about having situational awareness. He taught his daughter to stay safe in the world. One of the things that he taught her was that as you enter a new place, always take note of the exits. Don't just count on the way you came in as the same way to go out. Find additional exits and make sure that you are always close to one. If an emergency were to happen, don't go for the main exit where everybody else will be headed. That may even be the source of the emergency situation! If there isn't an alternative exit, you may even need to plan ahead.

In this conversation, another person (also ex special forces) spoke up who said that he had lived in apartments before that didn't have emergency fire escapes at the windows. Rather than counting on the various exits in the hallways, he would make sure that he had a ladder near a window as well as a rope.

I am sure that many readers can also recall a time when they were attending a social event with only the thought of going in their minds. How they were going to get there, who they would see, what they would do. Without having an exit in mind, you may have ended up staying a bit longer than you intended and find yourself regretting that the next morning when you had an early meeting.

Even people who have taken on a new job should plan their exit. Gone are the days when people would work at a company until retirement and leave with a pension account. Gone are the days where loyalty is rewarded. And gone are the days when an employee can expect to work their way to the top of the company. In a new job, you should always consider how long you plan to work for this company and what you expect to get out of it before leaving. This may not necessarily be time-based, but having a line in the sand as to promotions or promised benefits or other expectations is important. You should constantly be measuring your career against that decision so that you know when it is time to leave.

You should also have a plan for what you will do next. Will you change careers, or will you work for a competitor? Is there anything you should be doing now so that your exit plan works out in the best possible way for you? Perhaps you should be sure to get certain certifications or training. Perhaps you should work on developing relationships in your local business network. Being complacent in the day to day won't help you when things drastically change.

Likewise, a business owner should be planning their exit far into the future as possible. Aside from some of the situations described above, there are other implications that a business owner should think about such as tax strategies, family dynamics, health and long-term care, and other issues that may arise. Planning ahead will help the business owner maintain control over how the exit strategy plays out and maximize the benefit for everyone involved.

Having an exit plan is essential for any kind of venture you take on whether it's a new job, an investment, or even just a social outing. Knowing when to leave and how to leave a situation can be just as important (if not more so) as knowing when and how to enter. It's something that we should all take seriously and plan accordingly. Knowing when and how to exit can often mean the difference between success and failure.

Business continuity

Unfortunately, sometimes a business exit comes suddenly after a tragic event occurs that affects the business drastically. It is best to have plans in place that can help mitigate the risks of business closure. Business continuity planning is an essential part of any organization's disaster preparedness strategy. It is a process of creating systems and procedures to ensure the continuity of critical business functions in the event of a natural or man-made disaster. Disasters can come in many forms, from severe weather events such as hurricanes, floods, and earthquakes, to cyber threats such as data breaches, ransomware attacks, and system malfunctions. It could even be the incapacitation of a key manager or, perhaps especially, the owner. For organizations to be prepared for disasters, it is imperative that they create a comprehensive business continuity plan that outlines procedures for dealing with each type of disaster.

It is important to understand the risks associated with various types of disasters and how they may affect your organization's operations when creating a business continuity plan. This includes identifying key personnel responsible for decision making during an emergency, assessing potential physical and financial losses due to disruption of operations, understanding communication protocols during an emergency situation, and prioritizing essential functions that must be maintained during an emergency. Additionally, it is necessary to have detailed plans in place outlining steps for restoring operations in the event of a disaster.

It is also important to outline strategies for protecting data and information systems from potential damage or disruption due to a disaster or cyber-attack. This includes implementing measures such as backups on separate media (e.g., external hard drives), establishing secure off-site storage locations, regularly testing backup systems and processes, training employees on how to detect malicious software or phishing attempts (and responding accordingly), establishing monitoring processes for system security and integrity checks (e.g., anti-virus scans), and encrypting confidential data stored on computers or networks.

To further protect against disruptions due to disasters or cyber threats, organizations should create processes for obtaining needed supplies during emergencies (e.g., fuel, food). Additionally, organizations should develop relationships with partners who can provide support services during times of need (e.g., hardware repairs) and invest in reliable hardware solutions for mission-critical applications (e.g., uninterruptible power supply). Finally, it is important to consider implications related to remote work options during disaster scenarios – including policies regarding access control measures (e.g., VPN access) – so that employees can still work remotely while ensuring the safety of organizational information systems from potential threats.

Having the proper business insurance is essential for any organization to protect against potential losses due to disasters and other unforeseen events. Business insurance can help decrease the effects of a mishap, by providing coverage for property damage or loss, liability claims, and other financial hardships that may arise from an unexpected event. It also helps ensure continuity of operations in the event of an emergency by covering costs associated with repairing or replacing damaged equipment, as well as legal fees if necessary. Additionally, having proper business insurance can provide peace of mind to employees and customers who may be affected by an incident. Businesses are better positioned to handle whatever challenges they may face along the way by taking proactive steps to secure adequate protection for their organization's assets.

Having an accessible Business Continuity Plan (BCP) for all employees is an important step that organizations must take to ensure that they are prepared for any disaster or cyber threat. An accessible BCP ensures that all personnel have access to the necessary plans and procedures required to respond quickly and effectively in the event of an emergency situation. Without an accessible BCP, organizations are likely to struggle in the event of a crisis, resulting in costly delays and disruption. Additionally, having an accessible BCP allows for faster decision-making during emergencies by providing clear steps and instructions that employees can quickly refer to when needed. As such, it is critical that organizations ensure their BCPs are regularly updated, distributed, and implemented to minimize the risk of disruption due to disaster or cyber threats. Your BCP should be in your company-wide shared drives as well as posted in plain sight in areas such as break rooms, server rooms, and places where emergency equipment are stored.

Practicing your business continuity plan (BCP) at least annually is essential for organizations to ensure that they are adequately prepared in the event of a disaster or cyber-attack. Regularly rehearsing and testing your BCP ensures that all personnel understand their roles, responsibilities, and actions during an emergency situation. Additionally, running through scenarios helps identify any gaps within the plan as well as areas where improvements can be made. Doing so will help ensure that businesses remain resilient even when faced with unexpected disruptions due to disasters or cyber threats. Moreover, practicing the BCP on a regular basis gives employees confidence in their ability to respond quickly and effectively should an incident occur.

Implementing effective business continuity plans can help organizations prepare for various types of disasters by providing detailed guidance on how personnel should respond in emergency situations; protecting organizational data from cyber threats; obtaining needed supplies; establishing relationships with support partners; investing in reliable hardware solutions and allowing employees access to systems securely via remote access. Organizations must take these steps seriously if they are serious about being able to rebound quickly after experiencing disruptions due to natural or man-made disasters. The inability to handle a disaster can mean the unplanned exit of your company for you, your customers, and your employees.

Planning your exit

Exit planning is an important part of being an entrepreneur. Although often overlooked, it is one of the most critical steps in achieving success and maximizing returns for a business owner. An exit strategy outlines how the entrepreneur plans to leave their business and what they hope to achieve through that exit. It should include detailed information on how the business will be transferred, how the funds from the sale will be used, and what to do if something goes wrong. It also should specify when and why the business should be sold and how much it is worth. Entrepreneurs can ensure that their business has a definite end goal and that their return on investment is maximized by developing an exit plan early on. Investing time into planning for the future of your business should not be neglected - after all, it could mean the difference between success and failure!

Develop a comprehensive exit plan that outlines when and why the business should be sold, how it will be transferred, and what the expected return on investment (ROI) is. This should include details such as plans for future growth and potential risks. It is important to consider taxes, legal issues, and other factors that could affect the sale. Additionally, it is critical to establish a timeline for when the business will be sold and plan accordingly.

Research potential buyers for the business and decide if there is a preferred buyer or timeline for the sale. It is important to understand any laws or regulations that could have an effect on the sale. Additionally, evaluate any potential risks that could affect the sale. Doing this research should give you an idea of what kind of buyers may be interested in purchasing your business and help you make sure they understand the value of it before they start negotiations.

Have conversations with key stakeholders, such as family members and investors, to gauge their opinions and make sure they are comfortable with the proposed exit plan. This is especially important if family members own a stake in the business. Making sure everyone is on the same page as far as expectations and plans will save you time and energy in the long run. Additionally, be prepared to make changes and compromise if any potential problems arise.

Seek out advice from a qualified financial professional to make sure your retirement accounts are set up correctly and that you are taking advantage of available tax strategies prior to the sale of your business. This will ensure that you are maximizing the value of your business and receiving the most favorable tax treatment. Additionally, it is important to be aware of any potential tax implications related to the sale and to consider a variety of ways to structure the payment of the sale to minimize any potential tax liabilities. You can ensure that you are well prepared to maximize the value of the sale and to receive an optimal return on your investment by doing your homework and being proactive with the sale of your business.

Consult with a lawyer who specializes in business law to review paperwork such as contracts, leases, and other agreements related to the sale of your company. They can advise on any potential legal issues that may arise and ensure that you are taking the necessary steps to protect your rights. Additionally, they can provide guidance on issues such as confidentiality and non-disclosure. Taking the time to consult with an expert can help protect your interests and ensure a successful sale. All in all, engaging a business law attorney is an important part of the sale process and a wise investment for your company. With their help, you can move forward with confidence, knowing that all the necessary steps have been taken to ensure a successful sale. Remember, the sale of your company is an important transaction and should be handled responsibly. With the help of a professional lawyer, you can ensure that your rights and interests are protected throughout every step of the process.

Create an inventory list of all assets related to your business so that potential buyers can accurately evaluate its value before making an offer for purchase. This list should include information about the business's physical assets, such as equipment and furniture, as well as any intangible assets, such as patents, trademarks, and copyrights. Additionally, potential buyers should be provided with financial documents such as income statements, balance sheets, and tax returns so that they can accurately assess your business's performance and profitability. Assembling this information ahead of time will help make the sale process smoother for all parties involved.

Establish contingency plans in case something goes wrong during or after the sale so that you are prepared if anything unexpected happens down the road. For example, you may want to include a clause in the purchase agreement that stipulates how disputes will be handled and that outlines who is responsible for any potential costs associated with the sale. Additionally, you may want to consider setting up a trust or other legal entity to protect your assets in the event that something goes awry during the sale process. Establishing these safeguards ahead of time will give you peace of mind and reduce your stress during the sale process.

Representation and warranty insurance is a special kind of insurance that helps protect you if something goes wrong with the sale of your business. It can help cover costs if there are any unexpected problems. For example, if there are any issues with the accuracy of financial statements or other documentation that was provided by you to a potential buyer, the rep and warranty insurance can help cover those costs. Additionally, this type of insurance can also help protect you against certain kinds of legal disputes that may arise after the sale has been completed. This type of coverage is not required, but it is a good idea to consider obtaining this insurance if you are selling your business.

Create a marketing strategy designed to attract interested buyers by highlighting the strengths of your company's offerings, services, products, or technologies - this could include attending industry events or creating informational materials like brochures or videos detailing your company's offerings/advantages over competitors in order to stand out from other sellers in your space/marketplace when looking for potential buyers/investors). Additionally, establish a communications strategy that outlines how and when you will respond to interested buyers to keep the process moving forward. You can ensure that potential buyers have the information needed to make an informed decision about whether your company is the right fit for them by taking the time to create a comprehensive marketing and communications strategy.

Monitor market conditions closely so you can adjust your strategies accordingly if needed once negotiations begin with buyers/investors as market trends could impact both value offered for purchase and terms & conditions of said agreement/sale – look at comparable examples of businesses sold within same industry sector & geographic area (if applicable). Understanding the market conditions in your sector and area of operation can help you make informed decisions about when to move forward with negotiations, what terms & conditions are reasonable and what changes could benefit the overall sale. Additionally, by understanding market conditions, you can be better prepared to negotiate with potential buyers/investors if the need arises.

Consider involving a professional M&A advisor who specializes in exit planning – they can provide guidance throughout complex processes including negotiating terms and conditions, price setting expectations, getting deal closure quickly and efficiently; collaborate effectively with legal advisors & bankers involved in transaction; ensure compliance with legal requirements; act as middleman between parties involved (e.g. transferring current stock options); help identify any areas requiring further consideration or improvement prior to selling business and many other tasks.

Additionally, the right team needs to be in place to carry out your exit plans efficiently. Your wealth manager, lawyer, M&A advisor, CPA, and other members of your team should be well experienced and work well together. Each team member has their special function. A business broker helps people buy and sell businesses. An M&A advisor gives advice about buying, selling, or merging a business. An Investment Banker helps companies raise money by selling stocks and bonds to investors. They can also provide services such as helping with mergers and acquisitions, underwriting securities transactions, and much more. The right team members will help ensure that your exit plans are executed efficiently and effectively. Having the right team to ensure that your exit plans are carried out correctly is essential for any successful entrepreneur.

Remember that an exit strategy should not be viewed as a one-time event but rather as an ongoing process of planning and review. As your business changes over time, so too should your exit plan. You should periodically revisit it with your financial advisor or attorney to make sure that you have taken into account all relevant factors and that the plan remains up to date. It is never too early to start preparing yourself for the eventual end of your business - doing so will help ensure that you have the greatest possible chance of realizing your goals.

The end goal for any entrepreneur is to maximize returns on investment – an effective exit strategy will help you achieve this. You can ensure that your return on investment is maximized when the time comes by having a clear plan in place, including how the business will be transferred, when it should be sold, and how much it is worth.

Buyer types

Take into account what kind of buyers would be best to target as you start to develop a plan for selling your business. It's important to strategize a way to appeal to the right buyer in the same way that you developed a marketing plan for the products or services you currently sell. Three main categories of motivated buyers are Financial, Strategic, and Lifestyle. Financial buyers want to buy a business to make money. Strategic buyers want to buy a business so they can use it in their own company. Lifestyle buyers are people who want to own the business for fun or to collect passive income.

A financial buyer might be the best fit if your business has been increasingly profitable in the last few years. They know that they would get a quick return on the investment. A strategic buyer is a good choice if your business can give them a competitive advantage. Perhaps the market is flooded with your type of business, but there is one key differentiator that you've found and developed. A lifestyle buyer might be interested in buying the business if there's potential for passive income that needs little to no effort from the owner, such as a laundromat or camping facility.

It's important to consider the different types of buyers and determine which type would be best for your business. This way you can tailor your approach when it comes to marketing, negotiating, and closing the deal. You need to know what kind of personality and expectations you may be dealing with.

Also, consider how the potential buyer currently operates. A potential buyer may see your company as a good addition to their own company, rather than operating it as its own entity. Your company could be a perfect fit for a missing or weak piece in their company machine.

Customers or suppliers may want to buy your business. This is called Vertical Integration. Vertical integration is when a company buys another company that helps it with making or selling its products. For example, a retail store company might buy one of its manufacturers so that it can make more things itself and brand those items as the retailer. Consider that one of your best customers may want to take advantage of better pricing and quality controls or that a supplier may want more control over distribution.

Companies who want to come to your geographical area may want to buy your business. A potential buyer may want to enter the local market and buy your business for its customer base, workforce talent, infrastructure, and other resources. Buying a business with an established footprint would be a quick way to get into the market.

Companies with a large sales force may want to buy your business. These companies are typically looking for a product or service to add to the offerings of their sales team. Your business could be the perfect fit for them, and they may want to buy it to expand their portfolio and add additional revenue streams.

Companies with complementary goods or services may want to buy your business. A business that provides a product or service that is complementary to yours may want to purchase your business to have the full line of products or services. For example, a distillery may find it desirable to purchase a winery in the same area. These companies can combine forces to increase their overall sales and market presence.

There are many different types of buyers that may be interested when it comes to selling your business. It's important to consider the various buyer personalities and expectations you might encounter to tailor your approach accordingly. Whether a financial, strategic or lifestyle buyer is best for your business depends on its profitability history and potential competitive advantages. Additionally, customers or suppliers looking for vertical integration opportunities as well as companies with large sales forces or complementary goods/services could also become potential buyers. You can make sure you find the right buyer for you and craft an effective plan that will help close the deal by understanding who these prospective buyers are and what they want from the purchase.

Managing your expectations

I work with many consultants who work on either the buy or sell side in the process of selling a business. One of the most common things that each of them hear, regardless of industry or size of the business, is that the outgoing business owner typically has a bloated expectation of value for their business. As a business owner, you have been working hard to make your business profitable. You've put in long hours, worked through holidays, and may have even had your family volunteer work to get things done. You're proud of what you have accomplished, and you should be! You can physically point at things within your business and recall the blood, sweat, and tears that it took to get to where you are. Being a successful entrepreneur is an excellent accomplishment and anyone would commend you for the work that you have done and the value you have given to your customers and the livelihood you've provided to your employees.

Just like when a person has a garage sale and finally decides to let go of some of the family heirlooms, they quickly find out that emotional value doesn't translate to monetary value. Hang on to what you have accomplished. Be proud of the things that you have done. Don't ever let go of those things. But remember that you take sentimental value with you; it's not sold with the business.

***

Imagine if someone were to build a car. I don't mean rebuilding an existing car, but let's say they build a car from complete scratch. There's only one of them. It's a unique car with all the features and things about it that they thought would make the best car for any situation that they find themselves in.

Now let's say that you decide you want to buy this person's unique car. You see the value that it could provide you with and you like how different it is than any other car you see on the road. You start your due diligence and look at the car. You sit in the seat. You adjust the steering wheel in the mirror. You place your arm on the armrest and imagine yourself driving down the road. Everything about this car is great and you're pretty sure you want to buy it. You get out of the car and start talking price.

The creator of this car had been designing this car for eight years before even building it. They put a lot of work and thought into how to make everything just right. It then took several more years to build the car. They had to get the pieces custom built. It took trial and error. Hundreds of hours testing. Installing and replacing parts to make everything just right.

You aren't really interested in that. You want to drive this car off the lot and start putting it to use. You don't really care that there's been ten different sets of tires put on this car previously and it doesn't matter to you at all that this was the third iteration of the car's dashboard. It also doesn't concern you that the car been painted over multiple times until they found a color that was just right. You're not buying any of that trial and error. You're only buying what's sitting here on the lot.

The creator remembers all the time and effort that was spent. They're proud of what was accomplished and what it took to make this car. They've accounted for the wasted resources for previous iterations. The creator may price this car based on all of those things, but when it comes to the actual value, only the end result and the market demand matters.

*　*　*

Adam was the owner and CEO of an IT trade school that taught basic troubleshooting, network administration, and programming skills. He was passionate about helping people learn and grow, so he worked hard to make sure the school had the best teachers and instructional materials. The company was doing well and increased revenue year after year for its first 15 years. However, now on their 17th year, profits had become a bit stagnant.

Adam was never a risk taker. In fact, he had built his business from the ground up by being very conservative with investments and only taking calculated risks. So, when he heard about this new project that promised to revolutionize their industry, he was initially hesitant - but then the potential profits seemed too good to pass up.

He gathered his team members together for a meeting and discussed investing several million dollars into this project. The proposal was to integrate computer forensics into the curriculum. Everyone agreed that it sounded promising, so Adam decided to go ahead with the investment. He expected to get back all of what they put in plus more because of how much potential there was for profit.

Unfortunately, after months of hard work and dedication from everyone involved, things did not pan out as planned; the project failed miserably, and they ended up losing millions instead of gaining any value or return on their investment like they'd anticipated. Still, the project was now engrained in their offering and Adam refused to drop the curriculum.

In the years that followed, Adam began working with a Certified Exit Planner to sell his business. He had the idea that his company was worth a certain amount based on what other companies he knew sold for. He inflated that value because his school was the only one in the area that also had a computer forensics offering. He knew it was just a matter of time until that would gain more ground and become profitable.

After a few years of negotiation, Adam had to face reality. The program was a gamble, and it would be a gamble for the buyer of the school as well. It not only did not increase the value of the school, but it lowered the value due to the continued costs of teachers, classroom space, marketing, and administration. Couple that with the stagnant performance of new revenue and it was a harder sell than Adam had thought. His determination to get a high price for his school and unwillingness to listen to his advisor caused several buyers to walk away. Now, the problem only worsened, and the value of his company dropped since he engaged with the Exit Planner.

In the end, Adam had to accept a much lower offer for his business as buyers were not willing to take on the additional risk with the computer forensics program. The important lesson he learned was that taking risks can sometimes be necessary to find success and growth, but not all investments increase the value of your company.

* * *

Another thing to consider in the value of your business is the ability for someone else to run the business. If the business relies on your consistent involvement, it will have less value to someone else. Returning to our example of buying a custom-made car, you begin to think about how you might use this car. You ask yourself, "Do I even know how to get the oil change on this car?" "Can I take it to any dealership to get the oil changed or is it also customized in special?" "What happens when the computer modules fail?" "How do I troubleshoot them?" "How do I replace them?" You have a very specific desire for the kind of tires you like to use on your cars, are they even compatible with this car?

You ask the current owner if there is an owner's manual for this car. Surely, he's documented all the various parts that are on this car, where you can find replacements, how you can troubleshoot them, and who you can take the car to for repairs. The business owner stairs blankly at you and shakes his head. "No, it's just a car. It works. It's worked for me for years."

You now have two options. You know what kind of headache you're going to have if anything were to go wrong with this car. Despite the owner saying that the car is going to run very well for years to come, you have your doubts. You can either negotiate on price to cover the expected headaches that you're going to have, or you can walk away from the deal.

Buying and selling a business is no different. For a business to be successful, it must be unique. If you are buying a franchise and you already own one or two yourself, this may not be as much of a problem. Sometimes (less often than it should be), a franchise has documented policies and procedures that every franchise owner should follow. But especially if you are buying a business that was built from the ground up, you're going to want to have documentation on what makes that company unique, how it operates, what things may typically go wrong, and how those problems have been solved in the past.

From the start, a business should be run in a way to maximize the value of the company in a sale. It doesn't matter if you plan on leaving the company to your children or even just closing the doors one day and calling it quits. You never know what decisions you may make in the future and how those decisions may change over time. In some cases, business owners may find that health or family issues have caused them to sell the business before they had originally planned. The good thing is that if you have implemented the other things in this book, you are already well on your way.

What's next?

Having a plan for what's next in life after exiting a business is an essential part of being an entrepreneur. Having the foresight to plan for the future helps entrepreneurs make informed decisions that are not only beneficial for themselves, but also for their business.

First and foremost, having a plan means that entrepreneurs can focus on the present instead of worrying about the future. When entrepreneurs have a clear picture of what will happen after their exit, they can enjoy their current successes without anxiously looking ahead. This allows them to be more productive and creative since they're not constantly distracted by looming uncertainty. Furthermore, having a plan also gives entrepreneurs more opportunities to make sound financial decisions before exiting, such as investing in specific assets or taking out loans with favorable terms.

Having a plan provides structure and direction after an entrepreneur exits their business. It gives them something to look forward to and focus on while learning how to adjust to life outside of entrepreneurship. An effective post-exit plan can provide entrepreneurs with new skills, experiences and career paths that can help them transition back into regular life with ease and success. Having this kind of guidance also makes it easier for former entrepreneurs to maintain relationships with colleagues and customers who may have been affected by their exit — it fosters trust and ensures that everyone involved is taken care of during the transition process and beyond.

Ultimately, having a post-exit plan helps create a sense of security for entrepreneurs after they exit their businesses — it allows them to remain confident in the knowledge that they have thoughtfully considered every possible outcome and prepared accordingly. Entrepreneurs take control of their future while still focusing on maximizing successes in the present by planning ahead. This way, they can rest assured knowing that no matter what happens next in life, it will be well-prepared for.

Start another business - For many entrepreneurs, starting another new business is a great way to continue their entrepreneurial journey. After achieving success in one venture, they may find themselves with the resources and experience needed to take on another challenge. Starting a new business can also be an exciting opportunity for entrepreneurs to explore different industries or markets that are of interest to them. Plus, it gives them the chance to hone their skills and grow in ways that weren't possible before.

One reason why starting another new business can be beneficial is because it provides an opportunity for personal growth and development. Experienced entrepreneurs have already achieved success in one venture, so they know how to run a successful enterprise and understand what works best within their industry or market. Taking on a completely different type of project allows them to stretch out of their comfort zone while still building upon the knowledge they've gained from past ventures, which leads to further growth as an entrepreneur.

Starting up again also allows prior entrepreneurs access to more capital than ever before due to the fact that they have proven track records of success behind them already that investors feel confident in. This can be a great way for entrepreneurs to get their new venture off the ground and make it more successful than it would have been in its early stages. Additionally, previous successes also open more networking opportunities as other established professionals are likely to take notice of what prior entrepreneurs have accomplished and reach out to collaborate or invest in future projects.

Starting a new business is an exciting experience that allows entrepreneurs to explore different avenues of business while still having the security of knowing they've achieved success before. It's a chance for them to continue flexing their entrepreneurial muscles while gaining more varied experiences that could prove invaluable down the line. Having the confidence that comes from past victories makes starting anew that much easier and more rewarding.

A new business can be a great move for entrepreneurs who have already achieved success and want to continue their entrepreneurial journey. Not only does it provide the opportunity for personal growth, but also access to more capital and networking opportunities while still providing an exciting experience. There are endless possibilities out there waiting to be explored.

Invest in other businesses - For entrepreneurs who have successfully exited their business, continuing to build wealth can be a daunting task. However, one of the best ways for prior entrepreneurs to continue building wealth is by investing in other businesses. Investing in other businesses allows former entrepreneurs to leverage their knowledge and experience from running their own business, as well as benefit from the potential returns on investment that come with any successful venture. By understanding how investing in other businesses works, prior entrepreneurs can take advantage of this powerful opportunity and set themselves up for continued success after exiting their own business.

The first step when considering investing in another business is researching potential opportunities. This includes looking at things such as the industry landscape, current trends and customer needs within the sector being considered. Doing thorough research will allow prior entrepreneurs to determine if there are viable opportunities worth pursuing based on their particular expertise or interests.

Once a few promising investments have been identified through research, it's important for an entrepreneur-turned-investor to understand what type of return they should expect from each venture before committing funds or resources to it. A realistic expectation of returns should be established early on so that investors know what they are getting into and can manage their expectations accordingly. This also helps to prevent potential investors from getting into investments that are too risky for them.

Prior entrepreneurs should think about the types of relationships they want to create with other businesses through investing. Establishing strong working relationships with the management teams of companies being invested in can be a great way to ensure long-term success and ensure that there is mutual benefit between both parties. It's important for any investor to properly manage these relationships as they can often be the key to unlocking greater returns over time.

Investing in other businesses is a great way for former entrepreneurs to continue building wealth after exiting their own business, provided they take the right steps towards making informed decisions. Prior entrepreneurs should take the time to do their research, understand the industry and potential returns, and create strong relationships with those they are investing in. With these steps taken, prior entrepreneurs can enjoy long-term success and continue building their wealth in a safe and secure manner.

Educate others - For entrepreneurs who have recently exited a business, the sense of loss and purpose can be crippling. After having devoted so much time and energy to the venture, it is understandable that one would feel adrift without such an anchor in their life. Fortunately, there are many ways for an entrepreneur to find new meaning after exiting their business - one of which is educating or mentoring others about what they've learned through their journey as a prior entrepreneur. Educating others not only helps them gain perspective on the lessons learned from success and failure, but also allows them to give back in meaningful ways while regaining a sense of self-worth.

One benefit of educating others after exiting a business is that it provides perspective on successes and failures experienced during entrepreneurial pursuits. An individual may look back at decisions made during their venture with more clarity when considering what was known at the time versus hindsight knowledge gained later on. Additionally, by teaching these experiences to students or other aspiring entrepreneurs, they can share valuable advice based on hard-earned wisdom acquired over years of trial and error - helping those they educate avoid making costly mistakes themselves down the line.

Another benefit of educating others as a prior entrepreneur is that it can provide structure and purpose in life after exiting a business. Serving as an educator gives individuals the opportunity to continue to be an active part of the entrepreneurial community - something that many may have been a part of for so long. Additionally, teaching provides meaningful opportunities to network with other entrepreneurs and gain insight into current trends within the industry.

Former entrepreneurs can give back in ways they may never have dreamed of before by sharing knowledge gained from their experiences as a business owner. For example, helping someone else start or grow their own business brings immense fulfillment - while also being incredibly rewarding financially if done properly. Teaching also provides an outlet for creative expression, as well as a platform to share hard-earned lessons that can have an impact on everyone's lives.

Ultimately, educating others after exiting a business is not only beneficial for those being educated but also provides former entrepreneurs with structure and purpose in their post-exit life. By imparting knowledge gained during previous ventures, they can create new meaningful relationships and give back in ways they never imagined - while once again feeling the passion they had when first starting out. This can be incredibly fulfilling and rewarding - both emotionally and financially.

Enjoy your hobbies - Don't forget to take some time for yourself and enjoy your hobbies. After running a business for so long, it can be difficult to remember how to just relax and have fun. For entrepreneurs, life can be a roller coaster of highs and lows. While success is often celebrated with great enthusiasm, failure can lead to feelings of disappointment and even depression. After departing from your former company, you may be experiencing feelings of idleness and insignificance. One way to combat these feelings is by taking up hobbies that are enjoyable and rewarding in different ways than running a business.

One benefit of enjoying hobbies is that it allows an entrepreneur to step away from the pressures associated with the recent life changes. Taking time off or vacation days may not have always been possible depending on the nature of their venture; however, the opportunity to engage in enjoyable activities now can provide much needed relief from the stress of change and help you refresh your mind so your better equipped for tackling new problems.

Another advantage of pursuing hobbies is that it offers opportunities for personal growth through exploration and experimentation. When an entrepreneur is dealing with a life change, having an activity to turn to that allows them to explore new directions and interests can be immensely rewarding. Not only does this kind of exploration provide insight into what they may want to pursue in their business or career later on, but it also gives them the chance to grow personally and develop skills that could help them better manage future life changes.

Hobbies can also provide much needed social interaction for entrepreneurs who might not have as many opportunities for regular socialization due to their professional obligations. Having hobbies that involve other people provides the opportunity for meaningful conversations and interactions, which can create valuable connections with like-minded individuals and even open potential collaborations down the road. Such interactions can give entrepreneurs a sense of purpose and belonging, which can be just as important as achieving financial goals when looking for fulfillment in their lives.

Hobbies can also help entrepreneurs stay connected to their passions even during difficult times. It is easy to get bogged down with the stress of life changes, but having an activity that they are passionate about allows them to maintain a sense of joy and satisfaction. Pursuing hobbies can provide an escape from reality and remind them why they got into entrepreneurship in the first place. Plus, it gives them something fun and exciting to look forward to when things seem bleak.

All in all, engaging in enjoyable activities can benefit entrepreneurs who are dealing with life changes. Not only does it provide a much-needed mental break from the new pressures of life, but it also helps them explore personal interests and stay connected to their passions. With these rewards in mind, taking time to enjoy hobbies can be an invaluable tool for managing life transitions as an entrepreneur.

Travel the world - As a former business owner, dealing with changes in life can be a difficult and stressful process. But there is one way to make it easier: travelling. Travelling has been shown to have numerous benefits for people of all backgrounds, including those who are going through major life transitions such as retirement or starting over after a business venture. You can gain valuable perspective on your current situation and open yourself up to new possibilities that you may not have considered before by taking the time to travel and explore new places.

One of the most important benefits of travelling is that it allows you to take some time away from your everyday routine and reflect on what's happening around you. During periods of transition, our minds tend to become bogged down by worries about the future or regrets about the past; but when we take ourselves out of our comfort zone by visiting unfamiliar places and cultures, we can look at things from an entirely different angle – giving us much needed clarity and perspective on our current circumstances.

A second benefit of travelling is that it can help to restore our sense of purpose and direction. When life throws us a curveball, it can be hard to stay motivated and feel like we're on the right path. But when we travel, we are exposed to new people and cultures which can provide us with a renewed sense of inspiration and motivation to keep on going.

Travelling also offers us the opportunity to learn something new. This could be anything from picking up a new language or learning about a different culture, to acquiring valuable business skills or gaining insight into an industry relevant to our own. By gathering new knowledge, we are better able to plan for the future and make informed decisions which can help us succeed in whatever venture we decide to pursue.

Exploring new places can also open doors of opportunity that may have previously been closed off. For example, if you're looking for investors for your next business venture, travelling to foreign countries may allow you to meet people or hear about opportunities that you may have otherwise never known existed.

Travelling can serve as a form of therapy. When we take a break from our regular lives and immerse ourselves in different cultures, it helps us to reset our mental state and gain back our energy and enthusiasm for life. And who knows – you may even find yourself inspired to pursue an entirely new career after exploring the world!

No matter what life throws at you, travelling can be an invaluable tool for clearing your head and helping you move forward with confidence. So, if you're feeling stuck or overwhelmed by changes in your life, why not take the plunge and explore something new?

Take care of family - Sometimes an entrepreneur must exit the business because of family responsibilities, but it can also allow them to be more present with family than they were able to while running a business.

Taking care of family can be a helpful and necessary task and it's important to remember that this transition may be hard on them as well. It is not only beneficial for the entrepreneur's emotional health but also important to ensure that their loved ones have what they need to thrive. There are numerous ways that an entrepreneur can take care of their family during times of transition from providing financial support to offering emotional guidance.

Prior entrepreneurs can take care of family members when going through life changes by being available for emotional support and guidance. Whether it's listening to a loved one's worries or giving advice on how best to handle a difficult situation, having someone who cares nearby can make all the difference in terms of managing stress levels during tough times. Afterall, it's likely that you've gained quite a bit of emotional intelligence and wisdom while working with employees and clients.

Proven entrepreneurs can bring a sense of security and steadiness to their family during times of transformation, offering them the comfort they need. This involves taking the time to be present in the moment, ensuring that plans are made for the future, and having honest conversations with those around them. These actions help provide security and reassurance during an uncertain period and can make all the difference in terms of making sure everyone is taken care of. It's important to consider working with a wealth management planner prior to exiting your business.

***

Having an exit plan is essential for any kind of venture you take on. Understanding when and how to leave can be just as important as knowing when and how to enter. Having the foresight to anticipate potential outcomes and prepare accordingly, whether good or bad, will help ensure that your decision-making process results in success rather than failure. To this end, it is critical that you plan your exit strategy in advance to ensure the best possible outcome for yourself and those around you.

"Amateurs sit and wait for inspiration, the rest of us just get up and go to work."

— Stephen King, On Writing: A Memoir of the Craft

Building Frameworks

I discussed how a business coach may leave an entrepreneur feeling overwhelmed with their given homework earlier in this book. Similarly, in this book I'm offering you assignments, however, my goal is to assist you by constructing a leadership team and establishing an encouraging community for your success. I hope to leave you with accountability tactics and other frameworks that will help you to perform with a team of people rather than by yourself. Ultimately, you are responsible for your own success, but seek help and guidance from the teams talked about in this book.

Getting started

Step 1 – Take a thorough and critical look at your business as it is today. Write down all the areas in your business that need to be improved on.

Step 2 – Begin to develop your plans for the future. It doesn't have to be perfect.

Step 3 – Improve your strategy. This is a great time to get help from others.

Step 4 – Prioritize what you need now and what you will need to realize your goals.

Step 5 – Put your plan into action.

Step 6 – Measure your successes and failures.

Step 7 – Adjust and improve your plans.

Key takeaways

- Be consistent with your planning and actions.
- Utilize quality providers to help your business scale.
- Lean on the abilities, experiences, and knowledge of others to keep you on the right path.
- Take care of yourself, just as you should your business.

- Realize that you and your business are part of an ecosystem and that keeping that ecosystem healthy is good for your business.

Don't go it alone

Reach out to us at Frameworks Consortium. We have already systematized these frameworks so that you can hit the ground running. Our experienced team of strategists and business service providers will help you develop the right plan to achieve success. We provide our clients with the best solutions to their business needs. Learn more about how we can work together and make sure your vision becomes a reality by visiting our website at www.frameworksconsortium.com.

George Mayfield

Further Help

As mentioned at the beginning of this book, if you would like help with a specific business problem, you can email us at Info@frameworksconsortium.com or scan this QR code for a free 15 minute discussion.

Frameworks Consortium was designed to bring all the resources and practices of this book to the business owner. Our onboarding program is a comprehensive inspection of your business where we discover the most urgent gaps in your company now, as well as leading towards your strategic vision. Our C-Suite helps you prioritize those gaps and develop actionable plans to close them in the ways that is most likely to create value quickly.

Our exclusive group of Vetted Service Providers have proven to provide trusted services to our members at the highest quality. We vet these providers based on their experience, expertise, and dedication to delivering exceptional value to our members. With this network of experts, you can tap into a wide range of expertise and services that are tailored to your business needs.

Finally, to ensure that all components of our program work together seamlessly we have created an internal knowledgebase that includes all of our members' experience and best practices. This resource allows our members to maximize their success by learning from each other's successes (and failures). Together, the Frameworks Consortium provides you with a holistic approach to creating long-term value in your business. Let's get started today! Visit us at **www.frameworksconsortium.com**.

Mastermind workshops

Businesses often face challenging problems that require creative solutions. One way to help them solve these problems is by holding virtual or in-person mastermind workshops. These workshops bring together a diverse group of people, each with their own unique perspectives and skillsets, to brainstorm potential solutions and strategies. By tapping into the collective wisdom of the group, businesses can leverage this powerful resource to develop innovative solutions for any problem they may be facing. With the right combination of resources, tools, and techniques, virtual or in-person mastermind workshops can become an invaluable asset for any business looking to solve a complex problem.

Tiger team deployment

A Tiger Team is a group of highly specialized functional experts that are brought together to investigate and remediate a deeply rooted business issue. Financial, Technology, Culture, or any other discipline; we'll assemble and deploy an unbiased, highly skilled team of professionals based on your industry and type of issue you may have. We'll diagnose the root of the problem and recommend solutions, then work with you to put that solution in place. With years of experience working with businesses both large and small, our Tiger Team can help you find the best solution to move forward successfully.

Compliance projects

The scope of a compliance project is usually larger than you think. Companies usually have a limited budget to become compliance ready the first try, but an unlimited budget to do it right and pass. Be more efficient by working with our teams to pass your compliance audit in the shortest amount of time and budget possible. Our team has experience getting companies compliant in a variety of areas, including GDPR, SOC 2, HIPAA, PCI DSS, SOX and more. We understand the importance of properly documenting and verifying each step to ensure compliance with regulatory requirements. Let us help you become compliant quickly and efficiently by utilizing our experience and knowledge. Don't waste time or money trying to figure it out on your own.

Speaking

George Mayfield is an experienced and engaging public speaker who can bring his insights to your events. With a background in business strategy, competitive advantage, and operational development, he has the knowledge to help your organization reach its potential. His talks are tailored to the needs of each audience, ensuring that everyone gets something out of his presentations. Whether it's inspiring stories or practical advice on how to improve your business operations, George will leave you motivated and energized with actionable steps for success. He is available to speak at conferences, seminars, workshops, retreats, and other corporate events worldwide. Contact him today if you're looking for someone special to deliver a memorable presentation by visiting www.georgemayfieldspeaks.com.

Our Frameworks Consortium members are available for speaking engagements as well. With a wide range of businesses, expertise, and backgrounds we're sure to have the perfect speaker for your event. Our members are committed to sharing their knowledge and experience, helping your attendees realize their potential and set them on the path to success. Contact us today to learn more about how our speakers can bring some fresh perspectives to your event! Email us at info@frameworksconsortium.com.

Knowledge sharing

We're proud of the quality of research that comes out of the Frameworks Consortium. Our team has conducted extensive studies with our clients to continue to improve the services and delivery that we offer. Our white papers are available to clients to review and discuss with their management teams. They contain valuable information that can help teams make better decisions, both current and future. Our research is always based on real world examples and is the foundation of what we do here at the Frameworks Consortium. We strive to continually add value to our clients' operations and results.

Frameworks Consortium Publishing is an independent publishing organization that helps our clients and Vetted Service Providers share their knowledge through books, eBooks, and Audio Books. Our program offers resources to ensure their material is of high quality and offers valuable content. Visit www.frameworksconsortiumpublishing.com to learn more.

Frameworks Consortium occasionally hosts symposiums to offer business owners advice and resources. At these events, we share insights on current geopolitical and economic trends, industry shifts, and best practices. We also provide hands-on guidance on how to create effective strategies to manage changing conditions, optimize operations, and increase profits. We often bring in experts from other industries to provide cross-functional perspectives. Follow our Linkedin page to stay current on all our events. https://www.linkedin.com/company/frameworksc onsortium.

Becoming a VSP

Frameworks Consortium is always on the lookout for trusted business service providers to help our clients. We are continuously searching for the best suppliers with a proven track record and ability to deliver high-quality services as an official Vetted Service Provider. We seek out companies that provide flexibility, responsiveness, and value to our clients, so that we can help them succeed. If you believe your company has what it takes to become part of our network of trusted providers, please let us know! Visit our site at www.frameworksconsortium.com to apply.

Acknowledgements

I am deeply grateful to the many business owners I grew up around for their guidance, wisdom and mentorship which has been instrumental in my success. I was fortunate to be exposed to the business world from an early age, which allowed me to develop a deep understanding of how businesses operate and the principles that drive success. It is with this knowledge, my passion for helping others, and my commitment to continuous learning that I strive to make a positive contribution in all aspects of my life. As I continue to learn more, I always look forward to sharing what I have learned with those around me. My goal is not only to help people become successful but also inspire them to reach their fullest potential so they can create meaningful impact in the world.

I'm passionate about giving back and believe it's important for us all—no matter our economic status—to contribute in whatever way we can. Whether that be through volunteer work, teaching, mentoring, or donating time and resources to those in need, I believe it's our duty to make a difference. The world is ever-changing and it's up to us as citizens of the world to lead the charge of progress. We must all come together and share our knowledge, experiences, and passions for creating a brighter future.

I'm grateful for the opportunities I've been given throughout my life, many of which were made possible by mentors who took an interest in me and believed in me even when I didn't believe in myself. It's important to remember that success doesn't happen overnight; it requires hard work over long periods of time and dedication despite any setbacks along the way.

I am eternally grateful to Dr. Scott Sherman, professor at Texas A&M - Corpus Christi, who provided invaluable guidance and support throughout my college journey.

I owe a debt of gratitude to William (Bill) Sagert, who was the chief on-board the USS Kearsarge as well as Captain (retired) Steven C. Schlientz for having aided me in discovering my capacity to bring about transformation even in exceedingly resistant circumstances.

I want to express my deepest gratitude to Jon Hendricks, Andrew Walker, and Jared Krouge, who were the founding members of the "Spam Eaters of Yugoslavia". They provided me with unwavering support in my formative high school years and sparked the ability in me to bring together amazing people to do great things.

I acknowledge and appreciate the hard work of those who have helped me to create a powerful network; Sheryl Powers, Rob Bliss, Martin Metzler, Tom Allen, AJ Jordan, Russell Duckworth, Bill Wallace, Tim Nichols, Viktor Taushanov, Jack Kearney, Linsday Polyak, John Beaty, Paul Hittner, Ross Williams, Chuck Rogers, Steve Conwell, Doug Janowski, Keren Shamay, Clay Thompson, Ray Croff, Philip Goodrich, Brooke Dieterlen, Troy Patterson, Reid Johnson, Richard Cheng, Joe Santaularia, Jaime Hochhausen, George Handley, Jennifer Rose, Michael Battaglia, Kendall Castillo, Garrett Starks, Kimmy Wright, Stephen Snyder, Jolene Risch, Dustin Jones, Erin Gregor, Paul Arceneaux, Shei Unger, Jeannie Lewis, Juan Carlos Marcano, Kassandra Nordhoff, Chris Nieto, Randell Holmes, Alex Vantarakis, Joe Ruby, Dan Nye. Through these individuals, I have been fortunate to meet a variety of wonderful people both professionally and personally.

I want to express my heartfelt gratitude for the exceptional friends who constantly spur me on towards achieving greatness. Emily Ackerman, Cory Yeager, Chris "Honeycrisp" Honeycutt, Todd Cassell, Dagmar Metzler, Sezen Inci, Sabrina Turner, Shami Aliyev and family, Tom Dennis, Brett Scharff, Cheryl Smith, Maxwell Balsey, Madhav Surapaneni, Don Zelezny, Don Petty, Steve Schlichting, Ryan Roodenburg. This group of people is a huge source of strength for me, and I can't imagine going through life without them.

I am extremely grateful to all the business owners who have thoughtfully contributed to the formation of the Frameworks Consortium; George Burchlaw, Ben McGary, Rich Lyszczek, Justin Stile, James Lyszczek, Nick Ogilvie, Travis Springer, Lanay

Renstrom, John Allen, John Arnott, Vince Vittatoe, Jeff Shafer, Sean Rosensteel, Susan Bryant, Gerard Ibarra, Paul Feather, Eric Harrisson, Lynne McNamee, Doug Slattery, Jeff Sandene, Gary Vanbutsele, Dave Swift, Cary Clayborn, Marius Bratan, Drew Donahoe, Jeff Crilley, Jay Kingley, Art Hoffman, Lindsay Sakline, Jeff Wolfe, Ieshea Hollins, Valerie Grimes, JC Beltran, Scott Sterrantino, Tami Gilmore, Craig Sheef, Chris Jones, William Hartwell, Daniel Vermeire, Bill King, Grant Bellomy, Bob Hurtt, Cody Robison, Taresa Scott, Paul Polk, Bryan Flanagan, Sara Schroeder, John Almeida, Andrew Sterie, Kevin Wilson, Gerald McAdoo. Your generous aid has been invaluable, and I cannot thank you enough for your commitment!

I am deeply grateful to the individuals who enabled and encouraged me on my professional journey before I began building my own enterprise; Brad Retterath, Zane Barker, Josh Sadler, Kelly Hartley, John Volpi, David Lundquist, Matthew Bowers, Steve Roemerman, Paul Prien, Tom Abraham, Jeff Waldrop, Luke Escude, Chris Mata, Shane Lindstrom, Kevin Nguyen, Van Voung, Charles Campbell, Mikey Myers, Austin Moseley, Rodney Craig, Birju Patel, Joshua Propp, Randy Busch, Mark Shellshear, Ryan Schieb. My appreciation goes out to all of the incredible teams that I have worked with in the past; your dedication, hard work and enthusiasm have been key to our success.

I'd like to recognize the following veterans who have achieved remarkable success in their professional lives; Jim Hendley, Corey Vore, Jen Colby, T.C. "The Chief" Beckett, Logan Sutterfield, Chris Hoffman, Brandon Wong, Billy Cloud, Randy Watkins, Gus Cabarcas, Ryan Holloway, Larry Allen,

Jerome Hesita, Zach Mierva, David Seals, Ian Gregory, Frank Gustafson, Bryan Ball, Solomon Floyd, Matt Hinson, Bill Hale, Trea "Dank" Feist, Eknauth Persuad, Patrick Idom, Dana Perry, Rachael Ridenour, John C. Powell, Marshall Chapman, Jamie Bunetto. These individuals have exhibited exemplary leadership and commitment to their work, and I'm incredibly proud of their accomplishments.

I'd like to express my most sincere gratitude to our intrepid founding members, along with the distinguished C-Suite team that have followed them; Kent Barner, Craig Beck, Kim Koonce, Tim Kiernan, Glenna Hecht, and Kirk Coyne. Without their support, dedication, and hard work, the success of our organization would not have been possible.

I'm immensely grateful to Craig Duswalt, Ken Walls, and Laura Butler for giving me the motivation and encouragement to finish this book. They both have been a great source of inspiration and support throughout the process. Their influence and guidance have been invaluable along the way.

I can't express my gratitude enough for the hard work and dedication of our staff, Sunshine Vizconde and Jake Sloan, in making Frameworks what it is today. They are the backbone of our success, and I am incredibly proud of them.

Finally, I'd like to offer our sincerest appreciation for all of you who are dedicated towards making positive changes in your business, community and across the globe.

George Mayfield

Recommended Reading

Understanding Michael Porter: The Essential Guide to Competition and Strategy, by Joan Magretta. Harvard Business Review Press, 2011.

Wisdom of Crowds, by James Surowiecki. Anchor Books, 2005.

Team of Teams: New Rules of Engagement for a Complex World, by General Stanley McChrystal, David Silverman, Tantum Collins, & Chris Fussell. Penguin Books Limited, 2015.

How Boards Work And How They Can Work Better in a Chaotic World, by Dambisa Moyo. Basic Books, 2021.

Traction, by Gino Wickman. BenBella Books, 2012.

Principles: Life and Work, by Ray Dalio. Simon & Schuster, 2020.

Principles for Dealing with the Changing World Order: Why Nations Succeed and Fail, by Ray Dalio. Simon & Schuster, 2021.

Can You Really Think and Grow Rich?: Keys to Unlock an Extraordinary Life, by Ramy El-Batrawi. Independent, 2021

The E myth Revisited, by Michael E. Gerber. HarperCollins Publishers, 2004.

Love as a Business Strategy: Resilience, Belonging & Success, by Mohammad F Anwar, Frank E Danna, Jeffrey Ma F Chris Pitre. Lioncrest Publishing, 2021.

Scaling Up: How a Few Companies Make It...and Why the Rest Don't, by Verne Harnish. Gazelles, Inc., 2014

Glossary of Terms

Accountability Chart - An Accountability Chart is a visual tool that helps to clarify and define the roles and responsibilities of employees within an organization. It outlines the company's reporting structure and how each person fits into that structure.

The purpose of an Accountability Chart is to ensure that each employee understands their specific role in achieving the company's objectives. It shows how each person contributes to the organization's success, improving the overall efficiency of the company.

By using an Accountability Chart, a business can identify any gaps in its workforce or any areas where roles may overlap. It helps to keep everyone on the same page and reduces confusion when responsibilities are shared.

An Accountability Chart is particularly useful for startups or small businesses, as it ensures that everyone is aware of their role in the company's success. However, larger businesses can also benefit from an Accountability Chart, as it can help to create clarity and improve communication between departments.

An Accountability Chart is an essential tool for any business that wants to achieve its goals efficiently and effectively by enabling employees to understand their roles and the role they play in the company's success.

Actionable Strategy - An actionable strategy is a plan or course of action that can be implemented to achieve specific goals or objectives. It goes beyond just being a high-level plan and includes a detailed roadmap of steps and tasks that need to be accomplished to successfully execute the strategy.

An effective actionable strategy considers all relevant factors, including market conditions, competitors, resources, and internal capabilities. It should also be flexible enough to adapt to changes and challenges that may arise during execution.
Businesses use actionable strategies to guide decision-making and ensure alignment across various departments and teams. A well-defined actionable strategy can also improve communication, reduce inefficiencies, and increase collaboration among stakeholders.

To develop an actionable strategy, it is essential to gather data and insights to inform decision-making. This may involve conducting market research, analyzing financial data, and consulting with industry experts. Once the strategy is in place, it should be regularly reviewed and updated to ensure that it remains relevant and effective.

An actionable strategy is critical for achieving business success. It provides a roadmap for achieving objectives and ensures that resources are used efficiently and effectively to drive business growth.

Advisory Board - An Advisory Board refers to a group of experienced and knowledgeable individuals who provide strategic advice and guidance to a company's management team. These individuals typically possess industry-specific expertise, business acumen, and a deep understanding of market trends, which they leverage to help the company make informed decisions in achieving its strategic objectives.

The role of an Advisory Board is to advise, not govern. Members of an Advisory Board do not have decision-making authority or voting rights in the company, but rather serve as a sounding board for the management team. They offer recommendations on key issues such as market expansion, new product development, competitive analysis, and talent acquisition.

Advisory Boards are prevalent in startups and early-stage companies, where they can provide valuable insights and help founders navigate the challenges of building a business. They can also be found in larger companies, where they may advise on specific initiatives or help develop strategies for new business units.

The composition of an Advisory Board varies depending on the company's needs and industry. It may include industry experts, investors, former executives, and other professionals with relevant experience. The Advisory Board meetings are typically held quarterly or semi-annually and are aimed at discussing the company's progress and seeking input on upcoming initiatives.

An Advisory Board is a critical component of a company's success, as it provides expert guidance and advice to help the management team make informed decisions in achieving its goals. With the right mix of industry expertise and business acumen, an Advisory Board can be a powerful asset in achieving success and sustained growth.

Angel Investors - Angel Investors refer to high net worth individuals who provide financial backing to start-up companies in exchange for a stake in the equity. These investors can come from various backgrounds such as successful entrepreneurs, executives, or wealthy individuals with a keen interest in investing in new and promising ventures.

Angel investors are typically not interested in funding larger corporations or established companies, but instead focus on providing seed capital to start-ups and small businesses that have high-growth potential. They can provide not only financial support but also valuable mentorship and expertise to help companies grow and succeed.

These investors typically invest in companies at an early stage when they are just starting out and may not have a proven track record of success or strong revenue. In return for their investment, Angel Investors typically receive equity or convertible debt in the company. This means that they can become co-owners of the company and share in any potential profits or returns.

Angel Investors are an important source of funding for many budding entrepreneurs and startup companies. They provide funding when traditional sources such as banks or venture capital firms may not be willing to take the risk. Additionally, many Angel Investors have a personal interest in the companies they invest in, and their support can be critical to the success of these businesses.

Benchmark - A benchmark is a standard or point of reference against which other things can be compared or evaluated. It is a measurable and quantifiable standard that businesses use to measure and improve their performance. Benchmarks can be used to evaluate various aspects of a business including financial performance, customer satisfaction, employee productivity, and efficiency.

In the financial context, benchmarks are used to compare investment returns or assess the risk and return profile of a portfolio against a relevant market index. For example, a mutual fund manager may use the S&P 500 index as a benchmark to evaluate the performance of their fund.

Similarly, businesses can use benchmarks to evaluate their customer satisfaction levels by comparing them to industry standards. This can help businesses identify areas for improvement and enhance their customer experience.

Employee productivity can also be measured using benchmarks. For example, a business may set benchmarks for the number of sales calls made by a sales representative or the average resolution time for customer complaints by a customer service representative.

Overall, benchmarks play a vital role in helping businesses measure their performance and identify areas for improvement to achieve their goals and objectives.

Business Continuity - Business continuity is an important concept for any business in today's rapidly changing world. It refers to the ability of a company to maintain operations and services despite unpredictable events or disruptions that can occur at any time. Business continuity plans help businesses prepare for, respond to, and recover from unexpected situations such as natural disasters, cyber-attacks, pandemics, economic downturns, and other unforeseen occurrences.

Business continuity planning involves assessing potential risks that could affect the business operations; identifying strategies to mitigate those risks; establishing processes to ensure operational stability during times of disruption; developing communication plans with stakeholders; testing contingency plans regularly; and providing ongoing training on emergency procedures. The goal is to minimize downtime and financial losses by having a plan in place before disaster strikes.

A successful business continuity plan should include detailed instructions on how the organization will handle critical functions when faced with an interruption or disaster situation. This includes specifying which personnel are responsible for responding to different types of incidents and outlining specific steps they must take for services or products to remain available without significant disruption. Additionally, it is essential that all employees understand their role in ensuring the safety of customers' information as well as their own personal data.

Business continuity plans should be updated regularly to reflect changes in technology, personnel, regulations, and other factors that could affect the organization's ability to operate successfully. It is also important for businesses to invest in resilient infrastructure such as secure cloud-based services with reliable backups and disaster recovery capabilities. By investing in comprehensive business continuity planning, companies can be better prepared for the unexpected and have confidence that their operations will continue to run smoothly.

Change Control - Change control refers to the process and procedure of managing any modifications and updates made to a product or service within a business. It is a crucial aspect of project management and quality assurance, ensuring that any changes made to products or processes do not negatively impact their functionality or reliability.

In a business context, change control involves a well-structured approach to risk assessment, impact analysis, and approval procedures. This helps to minimize the risks of potential changes to a business's operations, including financial, reputational, and regulatory risks.

Effective change control strategies also ensure that all stakeholders are informed and involved throughout the change process, with clear communication and documentation at every stage. Furthermore, implementing robust change control procedures can help businesses to maintain compliance with relevant industry standards and regulations.

Overall, change control is a fundamental aspect of corporate governance, enabling organizations to manage risks, maintain quality standards, and enhance business performance.

Change Management - Change Management refers to the structured process of managing changes to an organization's processes, technologies, and systems. It involves implementing a range of activities that ensure a smooth transition from the current state to the desired state. Change Management is crucial in ensuring that organizations remain competitive and relevant in their respective industries.

The process of Change Management involves identifying the need for change, planning and designing the change, communicating the change to stakeholders, testing and implementing the change, and evaluating its effectiveness. Change Management involves working with employees, customers, and other stakeholders within the organization to ensure that the change is implemented with minimal disruptions and resistance.

Effective Change Management requires strong leadership, effective communication, and collaboration between all stakeholders. Organizations that do not manage change effectively risk facing resistance, low morale, and lack of engagement from employees, which can impact productivity and profitability in the long run. Change Management is a critical process that helps organizations adapt to changes and remain competitive in the ever-evolving business landscape.

It requires careful planning, effective communication, and collaboration between all stakeholders to ensure successful implementation and long-term sustainability.

Code of Conduct - A Code of Conduct is a set of guidelines and principles that govern the behavior of employees, managers, and other stakeholders within an organization. It serves as a standard of ethical and legal behavior, ensuring that everyone in the company behaves in a manner consistent with the values and goals of the organization.

A Code of Conduct typically includes policies and procedures related to areas such as discrimination, harassment, conflicts of interest, intellectual property, data privacy and security, and ethical decision-making. It outlines the expectations for behavior, provides guidance on appropriate actions and responsibilities, and sets the tone for the culture of the organization.

Implementing a Code of Conduct can have several benefits for a business. It can help to establish trust and credibility with customers, suppliers, and investors by demonstrating a commitment to ethical behavior. It can also reduce the risk of legal or regulatory violations, protect the company's reputation, and promote a positive work environment.

However, simply having a Code of Conduct is not enough. Companies must also devote resources to monitoring and enforcing their policies, providing training and education to employees, and creating a culture of accountability and ethical decision-making. By doing so, businesses can ensure that their Code of Conduct is more than just a document, but a living, breathing part of their organization that drives ethical behavior and business success.

Cognitive Bias - Cognitive bias refers to the tendency of individuals to make decisions or judgments that are influenced by their preexisting beliefs or personal experiences, rather than relying on objective data and facts. This type of bias can negatively impact various aspects of a business, including hiring processes, performance evaluations, and strategic planning.

For example, a manager might unconsciously favor certain candidates during the hiring process based on their similarities to themselves or their personal preferences, rather than evaluating each candidate on their qualifications and abilities. Similarly, a manager might give higher ratings to employees who share their work style, even if those employees are not actually performing better than their coworkers.

Cognitive bias can also lead to poor strategic planning and decision-making, as individuals may be more likely to rely on their past experiences or familiar approaches, rather than considering new or innovative ideas. This can result in missed opportunities, decreased competitiveness, and ultimately, lower profitability.

To combat cognitive bias in the workplace, businesses can implement measures such as blind hiring processes that remove identifying information from candidate applications, objective performance metrics that focus on measurable results rather than subjective evaluations, and diverse teams that bring a range of perspectives and experiences to the decision-making process. Businesses can improve their overall effectiveness and success by recognizing and addressing cognitive bias.

Compliance Standards - Compliance standards refer to the set of regulations, policies, and guidelines that companies are required to follow in order to operate within the legal framework of their respective industries. Compliance standards can cover a wide range of areas such as data protection, financial reporting, employee safety, environmental protection, and more.

Adherence to compliance standards is crucial for businesses as it helps minimize the risk of legal consequences, reputational damage, and financial losses. For instance, failure to comply with data protection regulations such as GDPR can result in hefty fines, while non-compliance with workplace safety standards can lead to costly injury claims.

To ensure compliance, businesses often appoint compliance officers who are responsible for assessing risks, establishing policies, and monitoring compliance activities. They also conduct internal audits and implement corrective actions to address any non-compliance issues.

Compliance standards are constantly evolving, especially with the increasing use of technology in business operations. Therefore, companies must stay up-to-date and continuously review their compliance policies to ensure that they are aligned with the latest regulations and best practices.

Consortium - A consortium refers to a group of companies or organizations that come together to collaboratively pursue a common goal or objective. This could involve pooling financial resources, technical expertise, or other resources to achieve a shared vision. Typically, a consortium is formed by companies in a similar industry or with complementary capabilities that recognize the benefits of working together.

Consortia are commonly formed to bid on large projects or contracts that require a significant investment of resources. By working together, consortium members can spread the risk and costs of a project while leveraging each other's strengths to deliver a higher quality result. Additionally, consortia can help companies gain access to new markets or customers that they may not have been able to reach on their own.

Members of a consortium typically sign an agreement that outlines the terms and conditions of their collaboration, including how profits will be shared, how decisions will be made, and what happens if a member decides to leave the group. These agreements are legally binding and help ensure that the consortium operates smoothly and fairly.

Overall, consortia provide a way for companies to achieve their business goals by working together rather than competing against each other. By leveraging each other's strengths and resources, consortium members can create a win-win situation that benefits everyone involved.

Cross-Functional Perspectives - Cross-functional perspectives refer to the concept of bringing together individuals from different functions or departments within a company to collaborate on a particular project or initiative. This approach aims to leverage the diverse skills, knowledge, and experiences of team members to develop solutions that are more holistic and effective than what any one individual could have achieved alone.

In a business context, cross-functional teams are becoming increasingly popular as companies look for ways to break down silos and foster innovation. By combining the expertise of individuals from different areas such as marketing, sales, operations, and finance, cross-functional teams can bring a multifaceted approach to problem-solving and decision-making.

The benefits of cross-functional teams include improved communication, greater creativity, and better decision-making. When team members with diverse backgrounds and skill sets come together, they are more likely to produce innovative ideas and solutions that may not have been possible through traditional departmental approaches. Cross-functional teams also promote more open communication and collaboration, which can help reduce misunderstandings and conflicts that may arise from working in silos.

However, cross-functional collaboration also has its challenges. It can be difficult to align goals and objectives across different functions, and team members may have different priorities or ways of working. Effective leadership and communication are essential to ensure that everyone is on the same page and working towards a shared goal.

Cross-functional perspectives are an important aspect of modern business strategy. By leveraging the diversity and expertise of team members from across an organization, cross-functional teams can develop innovative solutions and drive business success. However, effective collaboration requires strong leadership and communication skills to ensure that everyone is working towards common goals and objectives.

Deep Dive - A deep dive is a term used to describe a thorough analysis or investigation of a specific topic, project, or process. It is typically carried out by subject matter experts or a team of professionals who have extensive knowledge and experience in the area they are analyzing.

The objective of a deep dive is to gain a comprehensive understanding of the issue at hand, identify potential opportunities or risks, and develop strategies for improvement or mitigation. This type of analysis may involve collecting and analyzing data, conducting interviews, brainstorming sessions, or workshops, and reviewing documents or reports.

The benefits of conducting a deep dive include identifying hidden factors that may be impacting business performance, improving decision-making processes, enhancing operational efficiencies, and developing a more competitive edge in the market. It provides a holistic view of the entire organization and enables leaders to identify the root cause of a problem and take corrective actions to prevent it from happening in the future.

A deep dive is a powerful tool used by businesses to gain a comprehensive understanding of a particular issue, process, or system. It is a critical step in making effective decisions and driving continuous improvement within an organization. By enabling organizations to gain greater visibility into their operations, deep dives help to achieve sustainable growth and success in today's competitive business landscape.

Due Diligence - Due Diligence refers to the comprehensive and thorough investigation and research that is conducted by a potential buyer or investor into the financial, legal, and operational aspects of a company or investment opportunity.

The primary purpose of due diligence is to evaluate and verify the accuracy and completeness of the information provided by the seller or owner of the business, to determine whether the investment is a wise choice or not. This involves a range of tasks, including financial analysis, legal checks, background investigations of key personnel, market research, and more.

Due diligence is a critical step in the investment process, as it helps investors to identify any potential risks or issues that may impact the value or success of the investment in the long run. It also provides investors with the necessary information they need to negotiate a fair deal and make informed investment decisions.

Investors who fail to conduct due diligence may end up making poor investment choices, potentially leading to financial loss, legal disputes, and other negative outcomes. Therefore, due diligence is a crucial component of any successful investment strategy.

Emotional Intelligence (EI) - Emotional Intelligence (EI) is defined as the ability to recognize and manage emotions, both in oneself and others, in a way that enhances communication, teamwork, and overall performance. Higher EI in employees has been linked to increased job satisfaction, decreased turnover rates, and better decision-making.

EI is considered a critical component of effective leadership, especially in today's fast-paced and often stressful work environment. Leaders who possess high EI are better equipped to handle difficult situations, communicate effectively with their team members, and inspire trust and respect. They are also able to empathize with others, anticipate potential conflicts, and implement strategies to mitigate them.

EI can be measured through various assessment tools, such as the Mayer-Salovey-Caruso Emotional Intelligence Test (MSCEIT) and the Emotional Quotient Inventory (EQ-i). Many companies are now incorporating EI testing and training into their leadership development programs, recognizing the significant impact that this trait can have on overall organizational success.

EI is a crucial aspect of modern businesses, helping leaders and employees alike to effectively navigate interpersonal relationships and achieve company goals. By prioritizing EI development, companies can create a more positive and productive work culture, leading to improved employee engagement and overall success.

Enterprise - Enterprise refers to an organization or company engaged in commercial, industrial, or professional activities. Enterprises are typically created to generate revenue and profits by offering goods or services to consumers.

A successful enterprise is characterized by its ability to innovate and adapt to changing market conditions. It requires a combination of visionary leadership, strategic planning, and efficient operations. Enterprises must also have a clear understanding of their target audience and be able to effectively market their products or services to them.

In today's rapidly evolving business environment, enterprises must be able to leverage technology to stay competitive. This includes embracing digital transformation, using data analytics to make informed decisions, and employing artificial intelligence and automation to drive efficiency.

An enterprise is more than just a business. It is a complex organization with multiple functions and departments, all working together to achieve a common goal. Successful enterprises have a strong culture of collaboration, innovation, and continuous improvement, which is essential for long-term success in today's dynamic marketplace.

Entrepreneur - An entrepreneur is a person who starts and manages a new business venture, taking risks to make a profit. They identify a need in the market, develop a product or service to meet that need, and create a business model to bring their idea to life.

Entrepreneurs are known for their innovative and creative ideas. They possess the ability to see opportunities where others may not, and they take calculated risks to turn their ideas into successful businesses. This requires not only a deep understanding of the market and its competitors, but also a set of key skills such as strategic thinking, adaptability, risk management, and networking.

Successful entrepreneurs are often seen as role models and leaders in the business world. They drive economic growth and create jobs, contributing to the overall health of the economy. However, entrepreneurship is not without its challenges. Starting a business requires significant financial investment, time, and energy. It also involves overcoming hurdles such as market fluctuations, competition, and government regulations.

Despite these challenges, entrepreneurship continues to thrive and evolve, particularly in today's digital age where technology has lowered the barriers to entry for new businesses. With the right mindset, skills, and support, anyone can become an entrepreneur and build a successful business from the ground up.

Escalation of Commitment Fallacy - The Escalation of Commitment Fallacy refers to the tendency of individuals or teams to continue investing time, money, and effort into a failing project or decision, even when all signs indicate that it will not succeed. This fallacy is commonly observed in situations where there is a sunk cost, meaning that resources that have already been invested cannot be recovered.

The escalation of commitment phenomenon can lead to a variety of negative outcomes, including wasted resources, missed opportunities, and damage to an organization's reputation. It can also increase the likelihood of unethical behavior, as individuals or teams become desperate to salvage their initial investment.

While it may be difficult to avoid sunk costs entirely, business leaders can minimize the risk of escalating commitment by practicing effective decision-making strategies. This includes gathering all relevant information, remaining objective, and setting clear criteria for evaluating project success. It is also important to be open to changing course if early indicators suggest that a decision or project is unlikely to succeed.

Ultimately, recognizing and addressing the Escalation of Commitment Fallacy can help businesses make more informed and effective decisions, and avoid costly and unnecessary failures.

Executive Retreats - An executive retreat refers to a period of time during which top-level executives withdraw from their usual work environment to participate in team-building and strategic planning activities. Executive retreats are designed to enhance decision-making and to develop leadership skills, communication, and collaboration among executives of an organization. These retreats also provide a platform for executives to address pressing business issues in-depth, away from the distractions of the office environment.

Executive retreats are often held at remote locations, resorts, or other places that offer a change of scenery from the corporate office. During these retreats, participants usually engage in a mix of structured group activities, discussions, and individual reflection time. Some common goals of executive retreats include improving organizational culture, employee engagement and enhancing the effectiveness of corporate leadership.

The benefits of executive retreats are numerous, including providing a space for team building, facilitating brainstorming sessions, improving communication and interpersonal relations between executives, and enhancing the organization's overall strategic planning process. Successful executive retreats have been reported to lead to improvements in decision-making processes, greater collaboration between departments and a boost in overall company morale.

Executive retreats are an essential tool in modern business management, providing executives with the opportunity to bond, collaborate, and develop critical leadership skills. By taking a break from daily office routines and providing a change of environment, the executives can return to the work environment more refreshed, focused, and motivated to lead their organizations towards success.

Exit Strategy - An exit strategy refers to a plan put in place by an entrepreneur or investor to leave a venture or investment. It is a carefully thought-out strategy aimed at mitigating risks and maximizing returns. Typically, an exit strategy is executed when a business has reached a certain level of growth or when specific predetermined goals have been achieved.

There are several exit strategies available to business owners, including selling the company, taking it public through an initial public offering (IPO), or merging with another business. Selling the business is perhaps the most common exit strategy, and it involves finding a buyer who is willing to pay a premium price for the company. This may involve negotiating a deal with a competitor, another player in the industry, or a private equity firm.

Merging with another business can also be an effective exit strategy, especially for companies that are looking to expand rapidly. Mergers can help businesses achieve economies of scale, access new markets and customers, and diversify their product or service offerings.

Having a well-defined exit strategy is crucial for business owners and investors. It provides a clear roadmap for success and helps to ensure that the venture is profitable and sustainable over the long term.

Geopolitical - Geopolitical refers to the relationships between countries or regions, particularly in terms of their political, economic, and military interactions. It involves the study of the strategic significance of geographical locations and the political power and influence they have over other areas. The term also encompasses the study of international relations, including diplomacy, foreign policy, and trade relationships. Geopolitical considerations often play a crucial role in decision making by governments and corporations, particularly in areas such as resource allocation, territorial disputes, and alliances. Understanding geopolitical dynamics is essential in navigating complex global challenges, from climate change to international conflicts.

Key Performance Indicators (KPIs) - Key Performance Indicators (KPIs) are quantifiable measures used to evaluate the success or failure of a company or particular business activities within an organization. These indicators can be financial or non-financial and should be aligned with the company's overall goals and objectives. They are crucial for determining whether a business is on track to achieving its targets or not, and identifying areas that need improvement.

Some common examples of financial KPIs may include revenue growth, profitability, return on investment (ROI), and gross margin. Non-financial KPIs may include customer satisfaction, employee engagement, brand recognition, and social media reach. It is important to note that KPIs should be specific, measurable, achievable, relevant, and time-bound to be effective.

KPIs provide businesses with valuable insights into their performance, enabling them to identify areas of strength and weakness. By monitoring and analyzing KPIs, businesses can make informed decisions regarding resource allocation, strategy formulation, and goal setting. In summary, KPIs are essential tools for measuring and tracking business success and ensuring that companies are on track to achieving their objectives.

Mastermind Group - A Mastermind Group refers to a group of individuals who come together with a common goal to share knowledge, ideas, and strategies with each other. This group serves as a support system for each other, providing feedback and advice on various business matters. In this group, members challenge each other to set and achieve goals, hold each other accountable, and celebrate each other's successes.

Typically, a Mastermind Group consists of 5-10 individuals, carefully selected to ensure a diverse range of experiences and expertise. The group meets on a regular basis, either in person or virtually, and each member is expected to contribute and participate actively in the discussions.

One of the benefits of being part of a Mastermind Group is the ability to leverage the collective strength of its members. Members have access to a wide range of resources, networks, and knowledge, which they can tap into to grow and expand their businesses. By sharing ideas and strategies, members can avoid costly mistakes, learn new skills and best practices, and accelerate their progress.

A Mastermind Group is an essential tool for any business owner or entrepreneur looking to grow their business. It provides a supportive environment for personal and professional development and enables members to tap into the collective strength and resources of their members. Simply put, being part of a Mastermind Group can be a game-changer for anyone looking to take their business to the next level.

Niche - A niche refers to a specific and narrow segment of a larger market with unique needs, characteristics, and preferences that are not adequately met by mainstream products or services. This smaller and specialized market is often overlooked by larger companies due to its limited size and high costs associated with penetrating it. However, for small businesses and entrepreneurs, a niche can provide a lucrative opportunity to build a loyal customer base, differentiate themselves from competitors, and generate sustainable profits.

Identifying a niche requires an in-depth analysis of the market, consumer behavior, and trends. It involves understanding the pain points, preferences, and behaviors of a specific group of customers and designing products or services that address their unique needs. For instance, a company specializing in gluten-free products has identified a niche for health-conscious consumers with celiac disease or gluten intolerance who cannot consume traditional wheat-based products.

By offering a specialized product or service, businesses can charge premiums prices, reduce competition, and build a strong brand reputation.

George Mayfield

Additionally, a niche market offers a high level of customer loyalty and satisfaction due to the personalized nature of the products or services offered.

However, the success of a niche strategy largely depends on the ability of the business to maintain relevance, innovation, and quality of its products or services. The market is constantly evolving, and a niche business must adapt to changing customer needs and preferences to ensure longevity and profitability.

Objective Data - Objective data refers to information that is based on measurable, quantifiable, and factual observations. This type of data is free from personal biases or interpretations and is commonly used to inform business decisions and strategies. Objective data can be collected through various methods such as surveys, customer feedback forms, financial reports, and sales analysis. The use of objective data in business is essential for ensuring accuracy and minimizing the risk of erroneous decisions based on subjective opinions or assumptions. By relying on objective data, business leaders can make informed decisions, identify opportunities for growth, and gain a competitive edge in the market. Overall, objective data is a critical tool for any business looking to optimize its operations and achieve long-term success.

Organizational Health - Organizational health refers to the overall well-being and performance of an organization. It encompasses various aspects such as employee satisfaction, financial stability, internal communication, and leadership effectiveness.

Organizations with good organizational health have productive employees who are satisfied with their work, a strong financial position, and clear communication between all levels of the organization. They exhibit strong leadership skills and decision-making abilities that are supported by data and analysis.

One of the most critical factors that affect organizational health is employee engagement. Engaged employees are passionate about their work, feel valued, and are committed to the organization's goals. High employee engagement levels lead to better productivity, work quality, customer satisfaction, and ultimately, higher revenue.

Organizational health also plays a crucial role in attracting and retaining top talent. When a company has a healthy work culture, it attracts candidates who are looking for an environment that aligns with their values and work style. Additionally, satisfied employees are less likely to leave the organization, which reduces recruitment and training costs.

Organizational health is an essential element for a company to achieve long-term success. It involves creating a positive work culture that supports employee engagement, effective communication, strong leadership, and financial stability. Companies that prioritize their organizational health are more likely to attract and retain top talent, achieve higher productivity, and grow their market share.

Playbook - A playbook is a structured document that outlines a set of procedures or methods for addressing certain situations or achieving specific goals. It acts as a strategic guidebook for organizations, helping them to be more efficient, effective, and standardized in their activities.

Playbooks can be used in various departments, from sales and marketing to operations and human resources. For instance, a sales playbook can outline the steps to be taken when pursuing a lead or engaging with a customer, while an HR playbook can provide guidelines for employee onboarding, performance management, and workplace policies.

Playbooks typically include detailed procedures, guidelines, and templates that employees can follow to carry out tasks or make informed decisions. They can be regularly updated to reflect changes in the company's goals, processes, or industry trends.

The benefits of having a playbook in place are many. It helps to minimize errors, reduce training time, increase productivity, and promote consistency across the organization. Moreover, it can provide a competitive advantage by enabling companies to respond quickly and effectively to challenges or opportunities.

A playbook is an essential tool for businesses that want to establish a consistent and efficient way of doing things. It can help organizations to improve their performance, minimize risks, and achieve their goals with greater speed and accuracy.

Project Budgeting - Project budgeting is a critical process in any business that involves the estimation and allocation of resources required for a specific project. It involves identifying all the costs associated with the project, including labor, materials, equipment, and any other expenses required to complete the project on time and within budget.

Effective project budgeting allows businesses to plan and track their spending, ensuring that resources are used efficiently and effectively to achieve the desired outcomes. It also helps to identify any potential areas of risk or concern, enabling businesses to adjust their plans accordingly and minimize the potential for cost overruns.

In addition to ensuring that projects are completed within budget, effective project budgeting can also have a range of broader benefits for businesses. It can help to improve overall financial management, enabling businesses to better prioritize their spending and make informed decisions about future investments. It can also help to improve project outcomes, by ensuring that sufficient resources are allocated to each project to ensure success.

Project budgeting is an essential component of any successful business, helping to ensure that resources are allocated effectively and efficiently to achieve desired project outcomes. By carefully planning and tracking their spending, businesses can achieve long-lasting benefits that extend far beyond the immediate project at hand.

Quality Assurance - Quality Assurance, also known as QA, is a critical business function that ensures products or services meet or exceed established quality standards through a comprehensive review process. The objective of QA is to prevent defects, errors, or issues that could impact customer satisfaction, brand reputation, or financial performance.

To achieve this goal, organizations follow a set of procedures that involve quality planning, quality control, and quality improvement. Quality planning involves defining the quality objectives, identifying the quality requirements, and establishing the quality criteria for product or service development. Quality control involves monitoring the production process, verifying that the products or services meet the defined quality standards, and taking corrective actions if required. Quality improvement involves analyzing the performance data, identifying the improvement opportunities, and implementing measures to enhance quality standards.

QA plays a crucial role in various industries, including manufacturing, healthcare, finance, technology, and retail. For instance, in the manufacturing industry, QA verifies that products are produced with precision and accuracy, adhering to regulatory compliance standards. In healthcare, QA monitors the quality of care provided to patients, ensuring that healthcare providers meet the required standards and practices. In finance, QA reviews the accuracy of financial reporting, detecting, and preventing fraudulent activities. In technology, QA verifies that software and systems operate without errors, meeting customer expectations and industry standards. In retail, QA ensures that products meet the specifications and customer requirements, enhancing brand reputation and customer loyalty.

Quality Assurance is a business function that promotes customer satisfaction, brand reputation, and financial success by ensuring products or services meet or exceed established quality standards. An effective QA process requires thorough quality planning, quality control, and quality improvement, which are essential for various industries to achieve their goals and objectives.

Rational Analysis - Rational analysis refers to the process of making decisions based on objective facts and data rather than subjective opinions or emotions. It involves assessing and evaluating all available information, including financial reports, market trends, customer feedback, and industry research, to arrive at a logical and informed conclusion. Rational analysis helps businesses make better decisions by reducing the risk of biased or irrational thinking and providing a clear framework for considering various factors that can impact the outcome of a decision. It is a crucial tool for strategic planning, risk management, and achieving long-term success in competitive markets. Through the application of rational analysis, businesses can gain a deeper understanding of their operations and the external factors that influence their success, enabling them to make more informed and effective decisions.

Revenue - Revenue is a crucial term in business, representing the total income received from the sales of goods or services by a company in a particular period. This income can come from various sources such as sales revenue, rental income, interest income, or dividend income. In accounting, revenue is recognized when it's earned, regardless of whether payment has been received or not.

For any business, revenue is the driving force behind its success and growth. It's important to keep generating revenue to finance operations, investments, and future expansion plans. The ability to sustain revenue growth over a prolonged period is one of the critical factors in evaluating a company's financial health.

There are many ways companies can increase their revenue, such as expanding their customer base, introducing new products or services, increasing prices, or improving marketing strategies. However, it's essential to balance the revenue growth with profitability to ensure long-term success.

Overall, revenue is a significant performance indicator for businesses, as it measures the top-line growth rate and provides valuable insights into their financial health, market position, and overall competitiveness in the industry.

Root Causes - The term Root Causes refers to the underlying reasons or sources of problems or issues that affect organizational performance. These are the fundamental factors that lead to negative outcomes or poor results in terms of productivity, efficiency, profitability, customer satisfaction, or employee engagement. Identifying and addressing root causes is crucial for any business that wants to improve its operations, minimize risks, and achieve sustainable success.

Root cause analysis is a systematic process used by businesses to identify and evaluate the factors that contribute to problems or failures in various aspects of their operations, such as production, quality control, safety, customer service, marketing, or financial management. This analytical approach involves looking beyond the symptoms or the immediate causes of a problem and delving deeper into the underlying factors that create or exacerbate the issue.

Examples of root causes in a business context could be inadequate training of employees, poor communication among team members, outdated technology or processes, insufficient resources or budget, inadequate leadership or management skills, outdated policies or regulations, or external factors such as market changes, competitors, or political instability.

Businesses can take appropriate actions to address them effectively and prevent them from recurring by identifying the root causes of problems. This may involve implementing new policies or procedures, providing additional training or resources, upgrading technology or equipment, reorganizing teams or departments, engaging in strategic partnerships or alliances, or developing a contingency plan to manage external risks. The benefits of root cause analysis include improved efficiency, productivity, quality, safety, customer satisfaction, employee engagement, and overall business performance.

Sales Targets - Sales targets refer to predefined numerical goals or objectives that a company aims to achieve through its sales efforts within a specified time frame. These targets are set based on various factors such as past sales performance, market trends, competitor analysis, and the company's overall growth strategy.

Setting sales targets is crucial for any business as it helps in measuring the effectiveness of a company's sales team, identifying areas for improvement, and providing a clear roadmap for achieving growth objectives. Sales targets can be set at different levels, such as overall company sales, individual salesperson's targets, or team-based targets, depending on the nature of the business and its sales structure.

Sales targets are also tied to related metrics such as sales volume, revenue, profit margins, and customer acquisition. Sales targets should be SMART (Specific, Measurable, Achievable, Relevant, and Time-bound) and regularly reviewed and adjusted to align with the changing business environment.

Meeting or exceeding sales targets is a key indicator of a company's success as it leads to revenue growth, higher profits, and enhanced market share. Thus, effective sales target setting and management are critical for any business to remain competitive in today's dynamic business landscape.

Shared Value Model - The Shared Value Model refers to a strategy that focuses on creating economic value while simultaneously addressing societal needs and challenges. This model recognizes that business success is inherently tied to the well-being of the larger community and environment. An organization that embraces this model actively seeks out opportunities to create shared value by developing products and services that address social and environmental issues. Such organizations view social and environmental problems as untapped business opportunities and work towards creating innovative and sustainable solutions that benefit all stakeholders, including customers, employees, shareholders, and society at large.

The concept of Shared Value was introduced by Michael Porter who argued that businesses should go beyond traditional corporate social responsibility initiatives and instead focus on creating shared value in everything they do. According to Porter, businesses that create shared value are better positioned to meet the expectations of stakeholders, build resilient business models, and ultimately create a more sustainable future for all.

Several multinational corporations, including Nestle, Intel, and Unilever, have successfully adopted the Shared Value Model and integrated it into their corporate strategies. For example, Nestle's Creating Shared Value program focuses on four key areas: nutrition, water, rural development, and responsible sourcing. Through this program, Nestle has developed innovative solutions, such as fortified bouillon cubes that provide added vitamins and minerals to combat malnutrition in developing countries while creating a new market segment. Similarly, Unilever's Sustainable Living Plan has helped the company reduce its environmental footprint while creating new products, such as concentrated laundry detergents that use less water and packaging.

The Shared Value Model represents a paradigm shift in the way businesses approach societal challenges, one that places equal emphasis on economic success and social impact. By creating shared value, businesses can simultaneously address societal needs and business goals, leading to better outcomes for all stakeholders.

Shareholders - Shareholders are individuals, groups or entities that own shares or stocks of a company, entitling them to a portion of its ownership, assets, and earnings. In other words, they are the investors in the company who have a vested interest in its financial well-being and success.

Shareholders have several rights, including the right to vote on important company decisions, such as electing the Board of Directors, approving mergers or acquisitions, and making changes to the company's bylaws. They also have the right to receive a dividend, which is a portion of the company's profits distributed to shareholders on a regular basis.

Shareholders are a critical component of a business's capital structure, providing the necessary funds for the company to operate, grow and succeed. They are essential for raising capital, particularly in the early stages of a company's development. Additionally, shareholders play an important role in corporate governance, ensuring that management is held accountable for its decisions and actions, and that the company is being run in the best interests of its owners.

Investors consider a company's shareholder base when making investment decisions, as the composition and strength of the shareholder base can impact the company's operations and its ability to raise capital. It is important for businesses to maintain positive relationships with shareholders through transparent communication, financial reporting, and strategic decision-making to ensure their continued support and investment.

Software as a Service - Software as a Service (SaaS) refers to a cloud-based software delivery model where a third-party provider hosts applications and makes them available to customers over the internet. This type of service allows businesses to access powerful software applications without having to purchase and maintain expensive hardware and infrastructure.

SaaS is a popular choice for businesses of all sizes because it is cost-effective, flexible, and scalable. Typically, SaaS applications are subscription-based, which means that businesses only pay for what they need and can easily upgrade or downgrade their service as their requirements change.

One of the key advantages of SaaS is that it simplifies IT management for businesses. With SaaS, everything from software maintenance and updates to data security and backups are handled by the service provider. This frees up time and resources for businesses to focus on their core operations and strategic initiatives.

Moreover, SaaS applications are accessible from anywhere, on any device with an internet connection. This is particularly beneficial for companies with remote workers or distributed teams, as it allows employees to collaborate and access important information from anywhere in the world.

Stakeholders - Stakeholders refer to any group or individual that has a vested interest in the success or failure of a particular company. This can include employees, shareholders, customers, suppliers, and even the local community in which the business operates. Stakeholders play a crucial role in determining the trajectory and ultimate success of a company, as their needs and interests must be considered and balanced against those of other stakeholders.

Effective stakeholder management is key to ensuring that a business is able to meet its strategic goals and create sustainable value over the long term. By engaging with stakeholders and understanding their concerns and aspirations, companies can build strong relationships and harness their collective insights and expertise to drive innovation and growth. Moreover, involving stakeholders in decision-making processes can lead to better outcomes and mitigate potential risks or negative impacts.

Stakeholders in a business context are not merely passive participants, but active partners who have a significant impact on a company's performance and reputation. By recognizing and responding to their needs and expectations, businesses can build stronger and more resilient organizations that create value for all stakeholders, not just shareholders.

Strategy - Strategy, when it comes to business, refers to the long-term planning and decision-making process that organizations implement to achieve their goals and objectives. It involves analyzing the company's strengths, weaknesses, opportunities, and threats, as well as assessing the external environment, competition, and market trends. Based on this information, organizations develop a strategy that outlines a roadmap for achieving success and differentiation in the market. Effective business strategy requires a high level of semantic richness, which means using precise and accurate language to convey information. This includes identifying and defining key terms, using specific examples and data to support arguments, and avoiding vague and ambiguous phrases.

A well-designed business strategy can help organizations stay ahead of their competitors, anticipate challenges and opportunities, and achieve sustainable growth. It requires constant monitoring and adjustment to stay relevant and effective in a constantly changing business landscape. Thus, strategy is an essential component of any successful business operation.

Symposiums - Symposiums refer to events that gather a community of experts, professionals, and stakeholders to discuss a specific topic, share knowledge, and exchange ideas. These events can take the form of conferences, workshops, seminars, or roundtable discussions, among others. Symposiums are often organized by industry associations, academic institutions, or private companies to advance understanding and awareness of emerging trends, best practices, and solutions to common business challenges.

The main objectives of symposiums are to facilitate networking, collaboration, and knowledge sharing among participants. This is achieved through various activities such as keynote presentations, panel discussions, breakout sessions, and networking events. Additionally, symposiums provide a platform for companies to showcase their products and services, build brand awareness, and establish thought leadership in their respective industries.

The benefits of attending symposiums are numerous. They offer participants the opportunity to learn from industry leaders and subject matter experts, who share their insights, experiences, and recommendations. Symposiums also allow participants to meet and network with peers and

George Mayfield

potential business partners, which can lead to new opportunities and collaborations. Additionally, symposiums provide a platform for companies to demonstrate thought leadership in their respective fields, which can enhance their reputation and brand value.

Symposiums are an essential tool for businesses to stay informed about emerging trends, industry best practices, and new solutions to common challenges. They offer a valuable opportunity to connect with peers, experts, and stakeholders, and to gain new insights and perspectives that can help drive business success.

Value Machine (Value Chain) - Value Machine or Value Chain is a framework used in business management that identifies the value-adding activities of an organization. It refers to the series of processes a company engages in, from the initial production stages through to the final delivery of goods or services to a customer. This process involves designing, producing, marketing, delivering and supporting the product or service. The value machine is an excellent systematic approach for mapping out key business processes, which ultimately helps in achieving competitive advantage for the organization.

In simpler terms, the value chain approach helps a company in understanding their business and identifying the different opportunities to create value, minimize costs, and improve profits. This concept was conceptualized and introduced by Michael Porter, an American academic. The value chain is broken down into two main categories: Primary and Secondary activities.

Primary activities include inbound logistics, operations, outbound logistics, marketing and sales and service. Inbound logistics relates to the movement of goods, raw materials, and inventory into the organization. Operations refer to the production process in which goods or services are created. Outbound logistics involves the distribution of finished products. Marketing and sales involve advertising and the actual selling of goods or services, while service refers to after-sales support.

Secondary activities are not directly involved in the production process, but they provide support and optimization for the primary activities. Examples include procurement, technology development, infrastructure, and human resource management.

In essence, the value machine framework or value chain model enables organizations to identify which activities are the most valuable in their product/service offerings while ensuring that costs are being optimized throughout each step. Using the value chain approach, a business can assess its strengths and weaknesses, prioritize improvements, and build a more robust competitive advantage.

Vetted Service Provider (VSP) - A Vetted Service Provider (VSP) is a service provider that has been subjected to a thorough evaluation process to ensure that they meet certain standards of quality and reliability. VSPs can be individuals or businesses that provide a wide range of services, such as Web Design, Social Media Management, Bookkeeping, IT Services, or Recruiting/Staffing Solutions.

The vetting process entails checking the credentials of the service provider, including their qualifications and certifications, licenses, professional memberships, and insurance, among others. VSPs must also have a proven track record of delivering high-quality services to their clients. This often involves conducting background checks, reference checks, and customer reviews to establish their reputation and reliability.

Vetted Service Providers are preferred by many clients over non-vetted providers because they have been carefully screened to ensure that they are trustworthy and competent. This provides peace of mind to clients, knowing that they are working with a service provider who has been rigorously evaluated and whose credentials and qualifications have been verified.

Vision - When it comes to business, a vision refers to a company's long-term plan, goals, and objectives. It is a statement that outlines what the company hopes to achieve in the future and serves as a guide for decision-making and strategy development. A well-defined vision provides a clear direction for the company and inspires employees, customers, and other stakeholders to work towards a common goal.

A company's vision should be specific, measurable, and achievable, but also ambitious and inspiring. It should reflect the company's core values, strengths and unique selling proposition, while also considering market trends and customer needs. A good vision statement should be concise and easy to understand, yet also memorable and persuasive.

Having a strong vision is essential for business success, as it helps to align the organization around a shared purpose and sets the stage for innovation, growth, and competitive advantage. A clear vision also enables the company to attract and retain top talent, as well as win the trust and loyalty of customers and investors.

A business vision is a critical concept in business that defines the future direction and purpose of the company. By setting a compelling and achievable vision, businesses can inspire their stakeholders and achieve sustainable growth and success.

Wealth Management Planner - A Wealth Management Planner is a professional who provides customized financial advice and investment solutions to individuals or businesses to help them grow their wealth and secure their financial future.

Wealth Management Planners work closely with clients to develop a tailored financial plan that meets their individual goals and objectives. They analyze a client's financial situation, including their income, assets, liabilities, and risk tolerance, to provide personalized recommendations for investment strategies, asset allocation, and risk management.

These professionals also have a deep understanding of investment markets and economic trends, and they stay up to date on the latest industry developments to help clients make informed decisions. They provide guidance on a wide range of financial products, including stocks, bonds, mutual funds, exchange-traded funds (ETFs), and alternative investments.

Moreover, Wealth Management Planners work with clients over the long term to monitor progress toward financial goals, adjust investment strategies as needed, and help clients navigate life transitions such as retirement or inheritance. With their knowledge and expertise in financial planning and investment management, Wealth Management Planners play a crucial role in helping individuals and businesses achieve financial success and security.

White Papers - A white paper is a document that provides detailed information and analysis of a particular issue, product, or technology. White papers are typically used by companies as a marketing tool to establish thought leadership and demonstrate their expertise in each field.
White papers are also used to educate potential customers or stakeholders about complex products and services, and to provide solutions to common challenges.

White papers are typically written by subject matter experts and are designed to provide in-depth analysis and insights into a particular topic. They may include case studies, research findings, and technical specifications, as well as commentary and analysis from industry thought leaders.

The benefits of white papers are numerous. They offer companies the opportunity to showcase their expertise and thought leadership, and to differentiate themselves from their competitors. White papers can also be used to generate leads and establish credibility with potential customers.

White papers are an important tool for businesses to establish thought leadership, educate potential customers, and generate leads. They require a significant investment of time and expertise but can pay off in terms of increased brand awareness and business success.

About the Author

George is the Founder and Owner of Frameworks Consortium, an innovative consulting program that offers invaluable guidance to entrepreneurs and business owners. He has been in the industry for over two decades and his passion for helping people succeed comes from his personal experiences with family-owned companies and corporations alike, as well as from his time in the U.S. Navy.

George was born and raised in Mineral Wells, Tx, just an hour from the Dallas/Fort Worth Metroplex. He became a 3rd generation U.S. Navy Veteran, serving onboard the USS Kearsarge as a machinist (MR2). After 4 years and an honorable discharge, he pursued a college education, getting his Master of Business Administration at Texas A&M University - Corpus Christi.

George is an experienced professional who has worked with businesses all over the United States and several countries such as Mexico, Canada, Norway, Azerbaijan, Turkey, and Republic of Georgia. His unique approach to providing proactive, actionable advice makes him a sought-after consultant in this field. He works hard to ensure that every client receives tailored solutions that will enable them to reach their business goals without trial and error.

In addition to his work at Frameworks Consortium, George also gets involved in various community organizations dedicated to helping veterans and including serving on the board of a historic Texas rural church building. He is always looking for ways to give back and support those in need.

His dedication to pushing enterprises forward coupled with his commitment to giving back makes George a leader in his field. He strives to make the transition from entrepreneur to enterprise as seamless as possible so that small business owners can use their energy wisely instead of struggling through expensive learning curves or costly mistakes.

What people are saying about
FRAMEWORKS FOR BUSINESS SUCCESS

"This book is excellent for establishing and growing your business with practical, relevant, and important guidelines for success. Highly recommended read." – Laura Ann Margaret Butler, Career, Brand, & Business Coach, Keynote Speaker & Author

"I heard of *Frameworks for Business Success* by George Mayfield and was so impressed with its practical approach to navigating the ever-changing business environment that I recommended it to my international network of entrepreneurs. It will become a go-to resource for those looking to establish or grow their businesses from start-ups to established enterprises." – Shami Aliyev, Global Entrepreneur and Quality Assurance Director, Rabitabank

"If you're serious about your business and you want to take it to the next level, this book is your playbook. It's not just another business strategy book, it's a primer that's going to give you solid strategies that can really drive your company forward. The best part? You can go at it alone, using the book as your guide, or you can bring in the seasoned professionals - us, the Frameworks Consortium." – Kent Barner, Owner, CIO Suite

"George Mayfield has created an excellent and thorough 'how to' on building a successful business from scratch to exit sale. I love his business model and concepts because it goes beyond something just on paper. One of the biggest dangers in creating a business is the conflict you didn't see before you even started. George's business building formula provides business owners the best chance of a successful business partnership with the least risk of a costly partnership breakup" – Dana Garnett, Mediator & Founder, The Mindful Strategy LLC